I GOT
IT
FROM
HERE

A Memoir *of* Awakening
to the Power Within

~

FRANCESCA MIRACOLA

SHE WRITES PRESS

Published 2022
Printed in the United States of America
Print ISBN: 978-1-64742-483-1
E-ISBN: 978-1-64742-484-8
Library of Congress Control Number: 2022912619

For information, address:
She Writes Press
1569 Solano Ave #546
Berkeley, CA 94707

She Writes Press is a division of SparkPoint Studio, LLC.

Book design by Stacey Aaronson

All company and/or product names may be trade names, logos, trademarks, and/or registered trademarks and are the property of their respective owners.

All quotes are from *A Course in Miracles*, copyright ©1992, 1999, 2007 by the Foundation for Inner Peace, 448 Ignacio Blvd., #306, Novato, CA 94949, www.acim.org and info@acim.org, used with permission.

This memoir is a work of art based on my memories and how I interpreted them to heal. I wanted to share it with the world in the hope of helping others find peace. The names, locations, and some identifying details have been changed to protect the privacy of certain individuals.

Dedicated to my children ~
Cherish my love, forgive my fears, live in joy.

"Let me look on the world I see as the representation of my own state of mind."

ACIM W-p1.54.2:4

prologue

IT'S AMAZING HOW MANY ITALIANS CAN FIT INTO A DINING room on a Sunday afternoon. As a little girl in the 1970s, I took my seat at the kiddie table and listened to ridicule, intolerance, criticism, and rage ricochet from one relative to another. Instinct told me to grin and bear it, bide my time. I held out hope that one day, I'd rise above it and live happily ever after. But toxic patterns from childhood played out in my adult life. And trust me, it was no fairy tale.

"Did you hear Tony left Millie?" my uncle Mikey asked once as he reached for the antipasto. I was just a kid, but I knew my cousin and her husband were miserable.

"Can you blame him?" my cousin Sal replied. "She really let herself go," he added as he poured another glass of red wine.

"She'll never be able to find another husband," my godmother said disapprovingly.

"She won't be alone. Her fat sister isn't getting married anytime soon," my cousin said, poking fun at them behind their backs.

I took it all on as if the words came from me, or as if they were directed at me. Hunched over with vicarious guilt and shame, I ate with my head bowed and peeked up through my bangs, stunned that no one else seemed disturbed by any of this. The room spun from the sounds of laughter and the passing of dishes.

At the head of the table, my father dipped his bread in the homemade sauce and took his turn in the antics.

"Lily, these meatballs are worse than your hairdo," he joked. Dad had a knack for spewing cruelty under the guise of humor. "No wonder you're so fat, you're the only one who can tolerate your cooking." He shoved another forkful in his mouth.

"That's not nice." Aunt Luna half-heartedly laughed while making a meek attempt to defend her sister.

"Be quiet, Luna. No one wants to hear from a spinster." My dad's cutting tone sent chills up my spine.

He made fun of my mother, her family, and—at times—my brothers or me. His vicious jokes permeated the walls of our home long after coffee was served and the last of our cousins left.

After meals, my father retreated to the couch, where he sat with his legs crossed, hiding behind his newspaper. My mother cleaned up the mess. It never occurred to me that she was a person. She slaved over us, earning no appreciation or respect.

Even as a small child, I had a strong sense that the way my family behaved wasn't serving any of us. I longed to recognize this awareness in someone else's eyes in the hopes that I wouldn't feel so alone. But my relatives all seemed comfortable in the chaos, and I quickly learned it was best to follow along. My inner knowing became my dirty little secret.

The world outside our home offered me no relief. We lived in a neighborhood of identical brick townhomes occupied by my relatives, or friends who felt like cousins. Judgmental adults pointed their fingers at each other's families so as not to look at their own. I strived for perfection so they wouldn't point at me. I attended school in a uniform and conformed to the rules of the community. Yet, deep down I knew I didn't fit in. As I grew older, I worried there was something wrong with me.

It's no surprise then that my father walked me down the aisle and gave me away to a man I did not love. I was paraded past a church full of relatives who expected me to live the same kind of life they had, all while judging how I looked as a bride. Twenty-six years of familiarity with deep-seated dysfunction made it seem normal. I had a lot of doubts about my fiancé and my willingness to marry him. There were plenty of signs that I should run. Instead, I said, "I do."

chapter one

I WAS WILD IN COLLEGE. DRAMA AND ALCOHOL DISTRACTED ME from my anxious, racing mind. I pledged a sorority, because belonging to a tribe was the only way I knew how to exist. D Phi Z was filled with girls like me—Italians and Greeks from Queens and Brooklyn. I recreated my childhood on campus, hoping my mother wouldn't judge me so harshly. She despised an oddball, or worse, a snob. It irritated her that I attended NYU and lived in Greenwich Village. She wanted me home in my childhood room, enrolled at the local Catholic college that most of my neighbors attended. I pushed the limits, but only so far. Going home for the holidays meant taking a taxi over the bridge.

In 1992, my senior year, I reconnected with some old friends in a popular hometown bar to commemorate the night before Thanksgiving—the biggest party night of the year. We were moving between the past we thought we were outgrowing and the future we believed would be golden. We drank and danced until last call without a care for what time the turkey had to be in the oven— that was our mothers' concern, not ours. I kicked back shots of Jägermeister with Nicole, a friend I'd known since first grade. We giggled even as we cringed from the burning alcohol.

We set our empty shot glasses down on the bar and joined a circle of friends. "I don't believe we've met." A well-groomed guy in khaki pants and a button-down shirt shot me an unnerving stare. His jet-black hair had too much gel in it, a stark contrast to the preppy image he was trying to convey with his clothes.

"Frannie, this is my boy Jason," my childhood friend Dan chimed in. He clapped his buddy on the back and grinned.

"Nice to meet you, Jason," I said loudly, fighting over the music.

"The pleasure is all mine." He held his hand over his heart. He attempted doe eyes, but his eyes were too small and close together to pull it off.

We were positioned between the bar and the dance floor, and I felt the push of people trying to get by. Jason put his arm out behind me like a bodyguard blocking the paparazzi. "What's such a beautiful young lady doing in a place like this?" he asked. I humored him with a laugh, even though his pickup line was cheesy. He sounded like an old man. "Can I buy you a drink?"

"Oh no, that's okay. I just had a shot," I said, peering past him into the crowd. I was looking for Chuck, my high school sweetheart. Since the day we met at our lockers, we'd recognized something in each other, a warm feeling of, "Oh, there you are," as if we had known each other all our lives. We had dated on and off through high school and college but hadn't been in touch for a while. I was hoping to run into him that night.

"Something got your attention?" Jason moved his head until our eyes met. A hot blush crept up my cheeks.

"Sorry! I thought I saw someone I knew," I lied. "You can get me a water," I quickly added, feeling guilty about looking for Chuck, even though Jason was basically a stranger.

He motioned to the bartender. "Water for the lady, please."

"Thank you." I smiled coyly as he handed me the glass. I

wasn't attracted to him, but I was flattered by his interest in me.

The situation called for me to flirt. I was only twenty-one years old, but the pressure to be in a relationship was fierce. I'd had my first crush in sixth grade on a boy who didn't like me back. I chased him for years and made a complete fool of myself. I played that same chase out repeatedly, dating men who had no interest in a committed relationship with me, hoping to win their love.

Every romantic relationship began from my broken places, and each one added to my sense of unworthiness. I wanted to matter to someone so badly that I never gave a thought to what truly mattered to me. On the surface I was pretty, athletic, smart, and popular. I fooled everyone with my perfect image, but inside I was a mess. Now here was Jason, polished and acting like a total gentleman, gazing at me as if he'd found a diamond in the rough.

"Are you coming to our party?" I blurted. My friends and I were throwing a holiday bash in a couple of weeks.

"I haven't been invited," Jason replied.

"Well, I'm inviting you," I said, playing along.

"Then I'll be there." He smiled, pleased.

I immediately regretted the exchange. I heard a warning voice telling me to slowly back away. The voice frightened me, not so much because of what it said, but more because I'd heard it. It made me feel like I was a little bit crazy. I wasn't encountering a stranger in a dark alley, and Dan had seemed excited to introduce me to Jason. I dismissed what I heard inside, discounting it as the result of too many shots.

The band played "Our Lips Are Sealed." Nicole and another friend grabbed me by the arms and led me onto the dance floor. We formed a circle and bopped around like we were the Go-Go's, huddled together, air mics in hand, mimicking our best Belinda

Carlisle. Jason stood at the perimeter of the circle, staring at me as if I were the only person in the bar. His level of interest felt over the top and insincere. He caught my eye and, as if on cue, he feigned a look of admiration. But it felt more like a predator eyeing his prey.

~

Two days later, my phone rang. "May I please speak to Francesca?" It was Jason. My heart sank. I regretted giving him my number at the bar.

"This is Francesca." I didn't bother to fake enthusiasm. There hadn't been any sparks between us, at least not on my end. I had butterflies in my stomach when I met Chuck the first time. I can still recall the smile on his face and the sparkle in his eyes, the warm joy that bubbled in me just from being near him. Meeting Jason had felt nothing like that. I couldn't care less about seeing him again. In fact, the idea of it drained me.

"I was wondering if I could have the honor of taking you to dinner tomorrow night," he asked in his formal manner, which struck me as strange.

My entire body tensed. I wanted to say no, but knew I wouldn't be able to. As a child, being true to myself often got me in trouble. I learned at a very young age how to be who people wanted me to be.

"It's rabbit season," my older brother had once teased as he pointed a toy rifle at me, mocking the faux fur hat and coat my mother made me wear.

"I hate this coat and hat!" I sobbed in humiliation.

"Stop crying, Francesca," my mother scolded. "It's a very expensive coat." She wanted me to look a certain way in front of her judgmental relatives.

"I'm going to cut it to pieces with a scissor!" I screamed in frustration.

"Don't you dare!" She warned through clenched teeth. "You'll get a beating," she threatened.

My brother dropped the rifle, startled by the intensity of her rage, while I stood with my fists clenched in defeat.

I felt a familiar ringing in my ears as pressure built up to accept Jason's invitation to dinner. I looked around my room, desperate for an excuse to get me off the hook. A simple no was too uncomfortable for me.

"Sure," I forced out weakly and then winced with regret. I grew more and more frustrated each time I betrayed myself, believing I had no choice.

chapter two

I KNEW ON OUR FIRST DATE THAT SOMETHING WAS OFF WITH Jason. Bearing a bouquet of flowers and his plastic smile, he rang the bell of my parents' home. "You're more beautiful than I remember," he said, sounding pleased with me.

"Thank you." I gave a nervous laugh and shrugged off a chill sweeping up my spine. He was making such an effort to be charming, but instead of enticing me, it gave me the creeps.

He stepped inside and introduced himself to my mother, gently taking her hand and bowing slightly. "It's a pleasure to meet you," he said with an insincere smile.

My mother despised a phony. She shot him a look of disdain and said only a curt hello. I could tell she hated Jason, whose broad grin dimmed at her less-than-enthusiastic response.

Jason turned to my father. "Hello, sir. Very nice to meet you."

Impervious to the tension in the air, my father cracked a joke. Jason disingenuously lifted his hand over his belly and let out an artificial laugh. His robotic mannerisms were odd, but my father, who was only interested in himself, was pleased that Jason appreciated his humor. My mother looked like she was smelling something foul. She had keen emotional intelligence but could never articulate her true feelings without anger or judgment. I wanted to call off the date, but at the same time, I couldn't wait to get out of there. I left for dinner confused by my dampened spirits, not sure if it was Jason or my parents who'd caused it.

"Nice car," I said as Jason, like the perfect gentleman, opened the passenger door to the Mercedes convertible. I was naive and shallow enough to be impressed. I had no way of knowing that he'd borrowed it from his mother.

"It suits such a stunning passenger," he replied. "I made reservations at one of my favorite restaurants," he said as we headed off.

"Cool," I said, like a typical twenty-one-year-old. He was only two years older, but he chuckled at my response, leaving me wondering whether he found me adorable or unsophisticated.

We pulled up to the restaurant and left the car with the valet. Jason gently placed his hand on my back and guided me inside. The white tablecloths and candles didn't seduce me into thinking the place was any more special than other Italian restaurants I frequented.

"Jason, party of two," he said to the hostess. "I requested a table by the fireplace," he added, like a VIP.

Dinner was as stiff as Jason's body language. He was polite when he addressed the waiter, and he chuckled at my jokes, but there was no substance in his words and actions. He was attentive to me, but I felt unable to connect with him. They say the eyes are windows to the soul. I saw nothing in Jason's.

"Dessert?" he asked me as the waiter cleared our dinner plates.

"I'll just have a cappuccino," I replied. The waiter returned with my drink and a rock sugar stick.

"What's this, a lollipop?" I jokingly asked Jason. I'd never seen one before.

Jason snickered. "It's sugar to stir in the coffee."

My cheeks burned. "Ah," I said, embarrassed.

He patted me on the leg as if to say, "Good girl." I cringed. I wanted to slap his hand.

After dinner, he drove me home and walked me to my front door. I grew anxious, anticipating a kiss I did not want. Instead, he kissed my hand good night. "I would love to do this again," he said.

"Sure," I mumbled without meeting his eyes. He had just treated me to a nice meal, so it seemed rude to turn him down for another date. Besides, I could always make an excuse if he called again. It would be easier than turning him down in person.

But I couldn't say no, not even over the phone to a guy I didn't like. Jason and I dated for three years. Time and again, I said yes, despite myself, to dinners, outings, and intimacy. I wasn't attracted to Jason. I didn't even like him. My body tensed and my insides screamed danger when we kissed. But he worshiped me, telling me how beautiful and brilliant I was. He won over my friends with his charm, and we often went out on double dates or to parties with lots of other couples.

I liked the couples' nights the way a little girl likes to play dress-up in Mommy's high heels and makeup. I felt secure when we discussed a future together. Marriage was expected in my culture; no matter what I achieved, I would be a failure if I didn't get married. It was clever of Jason to recognize my weaknesses and capitalize on my fears. He lured me with the promise of lifelong security. I didn't love him, but I loved the idea of getting married.

Over the years Jason and I dated, I repeatedly found my way back to Chuck. We called each other or ran into each other at a club and picked up like we had never been apart. One weekend, while Jason was away at a bachelor party, I went to the Hamptons with some girlfriends. The summer sun was as strong as the drinks. The band was loud, and my denim shorts were short. I danced with a Long Island iced tea in my hand, showing off my tan more than my dance moves. Chuck appeared out of nowhere, a little buzzed, and we danced as if not a minute had passed since we were last together. The party continued into the night, and I wound up back at the rental house he shared with his older brothers and some friends. Going home with Chuck was as natural as breathing.

The next morning, I walked into the kitchen, where one of Chuck's older brothers was eating an egg sandwich. "Where did you come from?" he teased. I was like a little sister to Chuck's siblings.

"I hung out with Chuck yesterday," I replied nonchalantly as I grabbed a cold slice of pizza from the box sitting on the counter.

He shook his head and rolled his eyes. "You two need to figure it out," he advised.

It dawned on me then that my relationship with Chuck was complicated. The chemistry between us was as intense as our emotional bond. But he was immature, and I was dramatic. Chuck was a bit of a wild card, and I had no assurance of a future with him. I was afraid if I broke up with Jason and took a risk on Chuck, I would end up alone. I strategized and agonized over my future in an effort to ignore my internal chaos. It never occurred to me that I could exist on my own without a boyfriend. I needed the validation of feeling valued by a man.

∿

I graduated college with a reluctant desire to move out of my parents' home and into my own apartment. It's a natural step for a recent college graduate, but where I came from, it felt more like a blatant flip of the finger to my culture. I scoured the classifieds and even viewed a few apartments, but I couldn't sign a lease. I blamed my mother for not supporting my urge to go, knowing deep down I needed her to be the one holding me back. I resented her, but I resented my own cowardice even more.

I wanted my freedom as much as I wanted the safety of home. The only way out was to get married. Jason recognized my neediness and seized the opportunity. We planned our engagement while Chuck was out in clubs and seeing other girls. I didn't want to marry Jason, but Chuck seemed far out of reach. I was miserable in a relationship that I was afraid to leave. I couldn't relax and find peace in myself, so I kept moving forward on a path sprinkled with drama to distract me from my troubled mind.

When I sensed Jason was getting close to popping the question, I called Chuck. He answered the phone, and my stomach swarmed with butterflies. My heart expanded at the sound of his hello.

"Hey, it's me," I said. "It's been a while. I miss you."

"Well, you're the one in a serious relationship," he replied.

"You're the one hooking up with one girl after another in every club and bar in Queens," I shot back.

"But I think about you every day," he said softly. "I can't get you off my mind." There was a long pause. I nearly burst from holding my breath as I waited to hear what he'd say next. "Sometimes I think about showing up on your front porch and popping the question on the spot," he added.

Tears filled my eyes. I wanted to lose myself in Chuck, melt into him the way a child melts into a mother's embrace. The intensity of my emotions frightened me. Being vulnerable meant I might one day have my heart broken.

"I'm about to get engaged," I blurted.

"Then why are you calling me?" He sounded deflated, confused. Chuck didn't beg me to choose him. He remained silent, giving me the space to find my own answer within. His sudden maturity shocked me. I asked for a few days to think.

~

The next morning, I ran into my cousin's wife on the express bus to Manhattan. Barely twenty-five years old, she'd been married to my cousin for a couple of years already.

"Good morning, gorgeous," she exclaimed with high morning energy. She had a bubbly, flaky way about her, a whimsical flair to her soul.

"Hi, Gloria," I replied glumly as she slid into the seat next to me.

"What's wrong, cookie?" she asked.

"I'm caught between two guys, and I need to make a choice soon," I shared.

Bestowing the wisdom of a fairy godmother, she replied, "Follow your heart, my darling, not your head."

Sirens went off inside of me. The answer was not Jason.

The flash of clarity went dark as I rationalized. My fearful voice always seemed to speak the loudest. What did Gloria know? I was a CPA in a suit on my way to my important accounting firm. She was working in a department store, living the typical Italian girl married life. I wasn't going to wind up barefoot and pregnant in an apartment in Queens, married to my high school sweetheart. I was educated, professional, polished, and sophisticated. But my resume didn't match how I felt internally.

I called one of my best friends that evening to discuss my dilemma. Michele and I had known each other since kindergarten. She was top of her class in law school and dating a recent Yale graduate. Intelligent women from a generation with so much more freedom and opportunity than our mothers, the two of us appeared to have risen above our backgrounds.

"I don't know what to do," I whined.

"What do you mean, you don't know?" she exclaimed. "Chuck has no ambition. Your life will go nowhere fast. Jason's a law student. It's a no-brainer."

That was all the confirmation my ego needed. I wanted to move beyond my broken self and my ignorant background. I believed I'd have the chance to do that with Jason. He promised me our life together would play out like *Camelot*. My mother despised Jason and loved Chuck. I wanted an existence far superior to my parents'. I was trying so hard not to become my mother that I ignored the signs that Jason was far worse than my father. I ended it with Chuck and committed to Jason.

I should have committed to myself. But that was never an option.

chapter three

"YOU'RE GOING TO LET HER GO OUT WITH HIM TONIGHT?" I overheard my older brother Dominick ask my mother as I dressed for my New Year's Eve date with Jason.

"If she wants to be so stupid, then let her," my mother replied.

Dominick challenged my father. "And you're just going to sit there?"

"What do you want me to goddamn do?" Dad shot back.

The tension between Jason and my family had been building for weeks, ever since Jason had asked my father for my hand in marriage. This gesture of respect indulged my father's ego and duped him into thinking he and Jason were buddies. More than anything, my father cared about being held in high regard and well-liked by anyone outside our home. Without a thought for my well-being, or consideration of my mother's wishes, Dad gave Jason his blessing and then told my mother of the upcoming proposal.

She was not going to have it. She wanted me married, but not to Jason. Her desires were never acknowledged by my father. She resented him for betraying her while accommodating others, something he did frequently. He was Mr. Congeniality out in the world, but he degraded his family behind closed doors, blaming Mom and us kids for his unhappiness. In turn, she lashed out at him with savage rage.

This had been going on for years. When I was around seven or eight years old, my body trembled when I heard a dreaded yet familiar rumble signaling the onset of another vicious fight between my parents. I clenched the sheets up to my nose, wanting to hide while remaining vigilant. I wondered if my brothers were scared in their beds too. I contemplated making a run for their room but feared getting caught in the crossfire.

My parents moved from their bedroom into the hallway. Anger electrified them. The reason for the fight didn't matter; it always seemed there was something deeper at play. Their marriage was the perfect storm. Lacking introspect, it was where they played out their pain, resentment, and shame.

"You're nothing but a pig." I winced as my father insulted my mother.

"And you're a sissy like your brother," my mother shot back.

"You're a filthy slob like your sister."

"Your mother's a slut," my mother spat with vengeance. (As an adult, I learned my grandmother cheated on my grandfather while her young sons kept the secret from their dad.) Mom was so worked up she began to choke.

"Can't breathe? Is it your lungs?" my father taunted, then faked a cough. I cringed at his nastiness. My maternal grandfather had died from lung cancer.

"I'm going to dance at the funeral when your parents drop dead!" my mother howled. Her voice was low, deep, and threatening.

I crept out of bed and peeked out my doorway, frightened.

My father grabbed my mother and shoved her into the banister. "I'll fucking kill you," he snapped.

"Get the hell off of me." Her voice trembled.

"Stop it!" I burst from my room, unable to take any more. "Please just stop!"

My mother stormed into their bedroom and slammed the door, too angry to comfort me. She seemed helpless to free herself and her children from our plight. My father went from abuser to nice guy in a flash. He tucked me back into bed and tried to shush me to sleep, but I was more confused than reassured by his insistence that everything was okay. I couldn't trust my parents. I didn't feel safe.

An awkward silence filled our house for a few days until the fight blew over, and my parents settled back into their usual antagonistic coexistence. Their marriage was at best a convenient arrangement, typical of the time. Dad went to work and paid the bills while Mom took care of the home and us kids. They put up with each other for security; being in love was irrelevant. Their relationship felt dangerous to me, but their tolerance of it made me question my judgment. I was drowning in confusion, but I had no one to talk to. Survival skills I developed as a child hindered my well-being as an adult. Withdrawal led to isolation, the need for control bred anxiety, perfectionism brought about depression. Secrets gave rise to shame, and people-pleasing fueled resentment. My relationship with Jason was rooted in my brokenness.

My mother was unable to express her concerns about my involvement with Jason, or anything for that matter, in a supportive way. Loving, advice-filled chats weren't part of our family repertoire. Instead, she turned to what I thought of as her *Moron Manual*, an ethnic mother's guide of senseless rules imposed to perpetuate generational insanity. This manual isn't in print; it lived in my mother's head. In her world, there was a right and a wrong way to do everything, a protocol that had to be followed. How things looked on the outside mattered more than what was true. We constantly evaluated and judged others while fearing their judgment in return.

When she learned of my upcoming engagement, my mother flipped to a page in her mind and proclaimed that Jason couldn't propose. My older brother was getting married in six months, and our engagement would steal his thunder. We would also burden our relatives with two nuptials a year apart. I believe my mother had good intentions; she was trying to buy time in the hopes that Jason and I would eventually break up. I can still hear her say he was no good. She was wise to his manipulative charm and keenly aware that I did not love him.

My brother Dominick shared my mother's outrage. He longed for a well-bred life and saw the potential for this in me as well. Perhaps he believed our emotional pain could be cured by sophistication. He aspired to leave our neighborhood and culture behind us, hoping for a refined, drama-free existence. He desperately reached for it, but the *Moron Manual*, ingrained in him, always got in his way. Frustrated, he often exploded in anger. I judged him for his rage, arrogantly pretending I was above it, not recognizing he was trying to free us from the insularity of our relatives and community.

Dominick and my mom banded together like an angry mob, demanding my father go back to Jason and insist he couldn't propose until after my brother's wedding. Wanting to make sure he aligned with popular opinion, Dad went back to Jason, who refused to accommodate him. That ended their fake friendship. Irate at Jason's blatant disregard, my father joined the family crusade.

Over the holidays, I had become aware of the turmoil going on behind my back, yet we all pretended I didn't know, in order to keep the engagement a surprise. Our family dysfunction made me think Jason was normal; my relatives were the problem, although deep down I knew he was toxic too. I lost myself in all the drama. It was a safe way to hide from my own pain.

That night, a limousine pulled up to my house. Jason rang the bell and then waited on the front porch, grinning.

"I'm leaving!" I shouted, desperate for someone to tell me I shouldn't go.

"Take care," my father called from behind his newspaper.

"Bye, Francesca," my mother mumbled in disgust. I got the sense she was done with me. I pushed down the pain of falling short of her expectations. I told myself that somehow I'd win her back.

My brother retreated to his room once he realized my parents weren't going to stop me. His resignation made me feel deflated, like I wasn't worth the effort.

My sense of being abandoned by my family that night pushed me out the door. I joined Jason, telling myself that, at least in his eyes, I was worthy of love. I seemed to be a disappointment to everyone else.

~

Jason's plans for the proposal came together like a tapestry of scenes from every love story ever written. A limo into New York City, dinner at Sardis, *Phantom of the Opera* tickets, and a carriage ride in Central Park on New Year's Eve made for an unforgettably romantic tale.

I spent the entire evening anticipating the proposal. Marriage was expected of me, and I had pursued it with ardent determination. Jason was the means to an end. I ignored the doubts gnawing at me and tried to conjure exhilaration. I was going through the motions, faking joy in the hopes of finding it. I did not taste my meal, I wasn't moved by the show, and I didn't notice the beauty of Central Park. Everything was simply a backdrop for my expectation. I was waiting for life to happen, craving some impossibly perfect future because the present was a projection of my unsettled mind. The only thing I noticed was Jason's sly smile.

He didn't propose during the horse-drawn carriage ride through Central Park, the last activity on our list. *C'mon already*, I thought as we approached The Plaza Hotel. I sat on my hands, irritated that the night was a flop while passersby seemed energized by the pulse of the city. I resented Jason for making a fool out of me.

When the carriage stopped near our limousine, Jason got out and bent down on one knee. "Francesca, will you do me the honor of becoming my wife?" he asked. The moment was finally here, but my heart sank. I did not want a ring—not from him. My mind flashed on a string of self-betrayals over the years that had led to the present moment. I couldn't breathe. I wanted to say no, but I was in way too deep. My perfect image would be flawed, and those who judged me would be vindicated. At twenty-four, I was too afraid to take on the daunting task of being single again and starting over.

I covered my mouth, pretending to hold back a gasp of delight. I tried to shed a tear, but my eyes refused to go along with my deception.

"Yes!" I faked excitement despite being suspicious of Jason's motives, sensing beneath his charm a desire to control and manipulate me. The haunting similarity between the plot of *Phantom* and our relationship was somehow lost on me. I was book smart, yet naivete made me vulnerable.

Despite my reservations, I played the role of giddy bride-to-be so well it frightened me. Guilt flooded me. How dare I second-guess Jason when I was just as much of a fraud? That guilt triggered pressure to make it up to him. I would be a devoted fiancée, a good girl.

He slid a rock the size of a skating rink onto my finger. The moment called for a kiss, yet I peeked over his shoulder, more interested in the ring. The three-carat, brilliant-cut diamond sparkled on my slender finger.

We walked toward our limousine, where the driver was waiting with a warm smile on his face. He'd been given an itinerary at the beginning of the night, so he knew the special moment had just occurred. He seemed genuinely excited to be part of it.

"Congratulations!" he exclaimed. I connected to a warmth in his eyes that I did not see in Jason's. A wave of sadness came over me.

"Thank you." My voice trembled. Tears finally welled but not from happiness.

The joy in the driver's eyes dimmed. Young love should have offered hope in humanity and delight in the New Year. Instead, he was witnessing my despair.

"You okay?" he whispered to me as Jason reached into the limousine for champagne.

"Oh, yes—just shocked." I was well-trained in covering up my true feelings, but the driver was on to me. He sighed with disappointment, and I looked away, ashamed. I yearned to hug this stranger who understood me, but that seemed inappropriate. I would just have to suck it up and handle the consequences of my mistakes.

Jason handed me a glass of champagne. "To us." He raised his glass.

"To us," I replied. I sipped the champagne and pretended it was the start of a charmed life. We were a good-looking power couple on the verge of breaking the barriers of my narrow-minded background.

"I'm sure you want to show off the ring," Jason said. "I asked the driver to take us back to your neighborhood. I left my car at that pub you all go to. We can meet everyone there."

"My family will be there," I warned, suddenly trying to protect him, even though I desperately wanted to win them back.

"It's okay. It's your night," he insisted. My spirits lifted with the hope that all my wounds would be healed by our fairy-tale engagement.

~

We pulled up to the pub, and I stepped onto the curb like I was walking the red carpet. I mumbled a quick goodbye to the limo driver, unable to make eye contact, then waltzed into the bar, expecting to be the center of attention as the new bride-to-be. But the New Year's Eve party was well underway, and my entrance went unnoticed. The bar area was packed with people, some wearing 1996 hats, all with drinks in their hands. The music was loud, but the drunk chatter and laughter were even louder. I scanned the crowd, waiting for someone to notice me. Finally, my eyes met Nicole's.

"Happy New Year, Frannie!" she shouted before blowing her horn.

"Happy New Year," I replied, holding out my hand.

"Holy crap, congratulations!" she howled.

"Frannie got engaged!" she screamed to our circle of friends.

Jason and I were flooded with congratulatory hugs from buzzed friends who oohed and ahed at the ring. My brothers were there too. They did not acknowledge us.

The support of well-wishers lasted only a few moments. The high from the spotlight quickly wore off when everyone turned their attention back to the party. I looked around, itching for another rush. My mother was glaring at me from the dining area, where she was sitting with my father and their friends. As usual, Dad was chatting enthusiastically with anyone who would listen.

"There are my parents." I grabbed Jason by the arm.

I approached them slowly, fussing with my skirt and my hair. "Happy New Year," I cautiously said to my mom.

"Happy New Year," she flatly replied.

"I got engaged," I half stated, half questioned as I held out my hand.

"That's nice. Congratulations." She didn't acknowledge Jason, who stood stiffly by my side.

I lowered my head and stared at my shoes. My mind raced for a way to make it better. Maybe I could break through to my father. He seemed in good spirits, dressed up and surrounded by friends who thought he was a great guy. I looked over at him, but he turned his back to Jason and me, acting like a tough guy, when in reality he was a coward. He didn't care about our engagement, my brother's wedding, my mother's anger, or me. He always aligned himself with whatever cause kept him most popular. My brothers and I had spent our childhoods competing with each other to be the one Dad loved most, alternating between being the prize child and the problem.

My friend Michele, the one who'd insisted Jason was a better choice than Chuck, had followed us toward my parents. She was hoping to witness the exciting moment and share in my joy. Instead, tears filled her eyes. I pulled her outside. She didn't seem to notice the frigid January air.

"I can't believe how mean and coldhearted they're being," she said, sobbing. "They should be so excited for you."

"It's okay." I comforted her, shivering. I had left my coat inside. "I don't care what they think," I added with feigned confidence. Soothing her gave me a false sense of strength. I smiled at a couple who walked out of the bar, grabbed the door from them, and ushered Michele back in.

In the bar I paused, awkwardly aware of myself as if I had stumbled onto a movie set, yet no one seemed to notice me. Nervous energy bubbled as I tried to act as happy as everyone else looked. I sat on a barstool near Jason, who stood smoking a cigar. The smoke nauseated me, but that never stopped him. I asked the bartender for a glass of water. I sighed, weighed down by drama and resigned to the fact that my life would always be complicated. Dysfunction was my birthright. I gave up any hope of living in peace.

I noticed my parents gathering their coats, and suddenly I feared being left behind.

"I'm ready to go." I put down my glass and grabbed my purse.

"Why the rush?" Jason asked.

"I'm just really tired." As I said the words, I realized it was true. I was exhausted by my family, Jason's plans, and my facade.

"Let me just finish my cigar," he said.

"Oh, you do that, no rush," I said. "Stay and have fun. My parents can drive me home."

"If that's what you want." His nostrils flared, a signal I'd learned indicated his disapproval. But I was free to go. I hurried to catch up to my parents.

We drove home in silence, my mother seething alongside my oblivious father. I sat in the back seat like a child, fidgeting with the ring. I had struggled to do everything that was expected of me, but I'd failed miserably. I stared out the window, wondering how I would fix this mess and gain my parents' love and approval.

chapter four

EIGHTEEN MONTHS IS A LONG ENGAGEMENT PERIOD WHEN YOU aren't in love with your fiancé. I persevered. Enduring a bad relationship seemed easier than being left out of the marriage culture that surrounded me. To others, Jason and I appeared to get along well. But below the surface lurked abuse. He grabbed my ass as we slow danced at my friend's Disney destination wedding. It was a gesture that would have made me uncomfortable behind closed doors, let alone on a dance floor at an afternoon wedding. I shoved his hand away. The rejection triggered his rage. He didn't lash out in the moment—he wouldn't risk exposing himself in front of my friends—but I sensed from his tight jaw and flared nostrils that I'd pay for it later.

After the reception, we returned to our hotel room to change before meeting up with friends to enjoy the theme parks. I rummaged through my suitcase to grab a change of clothes, trying to ignore the tension in the air, while Jason sat stiffly on the edge of the bed.

"How dare you humiliate me like that at the reception?" he asked, seething as he stood and blocked me from entering the bathroom to change. He wasn't very tall, but his stocky frame overpowered my slender build.

"I didn't mean to humiliate you. It just made me uncomfortable in front of the other guests." I dreaded his anger. I tried to slip by him into the bathroom, but he pressed his shoulder into my chest.

"I don't care about the other guests. You're my fiancée. I can touch you however I want to." He was bullying me.

"No, you can't." My tone changed from appeasing to indignation.

"Oh yeah?' He shoved me.

"Leave me alone!" I shoved him back. It was a rare moment when my dignity mattered more than pretenses.

He grabbed my arm. "Don't ever defy me again," he warned as he turned me around and pinned me to the wall. He grabbed my ass just like he had done on the dance floor.

"You're a psycho," I yelled, one cheek squished to the wall.

He spun me around to face him and held me by the throat. "Don't tempt me." His lower jaw locked, and his eyes set on mine, flashing a warning.

I froze, not quite believing things had gotten so bad. He held me there for a bit, asserting his dominance. Once he was satisfied that he'd put me in my place, he released his grip.

I trembled with fear and hatred as I finished getting ready to meet my friends at the shuttle bus. I summoned the strength to go numb and block it out. My fear of falling apart was stronger than my fear of physical abuse. We joined everyone as if nothing had happened. I was used to normalizing bad behavior; I'd seen my parents do it my whole life.

After an episode like that, Jason would turn on the charm and go out of his way to dote on me, sucking me back in until the next time. He knew how insecure and desperate I was. Instead of leaving him, I tiptoed around him, painstakingly trying not to rile the monster. I tolerated physical and emotional abuse and downplayed toxic behavior because it was so important to be in a relationship. I felt immense pressure from my extended family and my culture to get married. My friends were all in serious relationships, engaged, or married. I was such an emotional mess that I feared I might not ever find another guy. I distracted myself by focusing on the wedding plans instead of on the relationship.

Dealing with Jason felt like maneuvering through a minefield. He had a tendency to hold a grudge and patiently wait for his revenge. When my car broke down one day by the Throgs Neck Bridge, I called him. "Can you please come and get me?" I asked.

There was a long pause. Finally he said, "Why don't you call Chuck?"

"What?" I asked, dumbfounded. "I haven't spoken with Chuck in months. Are you serious?"

"As a heart attack." He hung up, leaving me to find some other way home. He hadn't brought Chuck up to me before; he let his jealousy fester until he had the chance to punish me.

Jason had a way of making me feel like his abuse was my fault. He was especially good at convincing me that he was the victim of my family's hatred. The relationship between them worsened during our engagement. Dominick tried to forbid Jason from attending his wedding, and I had to beg my brother to allow my fiancé to come. I desperately wanted everything to be normal. My brother eventually caved, at my parents' request. They only wanted to save face. Jason wasn't part of the wedding, nor did he and I share any sense of connection.

As if dealing with Jason wasn't enough, I had to deal with his mother too. When Jason and I started dating, Joanne gushed that I was the girl she dreamed her darling son would find. Just like Jason, she went on and on to anyone who would listen about how beautiful I was, how brilliant I was, and what an impressive career path I was on. She played up the good-looking power-couple fantasy. But I sensed something was very wrong with all of her attention to our relationship.

Jason's parents divorced when he was a young boy. When his dad moved out, Jason was told he was the man of the house. He had a volatile, sporadic relationship with his dad, primarily based on his mom's feelings toward his father at any given time.

Jason and his mother had a relationship that felt inappropriate to me. He lived with her, his stepdad, and his brother. Once when I stopped by there, Joanne stepped out of the shower and into the living room with only a small towel wrapped around her. She chatted with Jason, dripping wet, right in front of me. He didn't seem to think anything of her suggestive behavior, her lack of boundaries. They referred to each other as "gorgeous" and "handsome." She often had her hand on his lapel, her head nuzzled against his neck. He would cup his hands over her face and kiss her head like she was the love of his life. She soaked up the attention she received from him.

Jason's brother Gavin, younger by only a year, once told me I was his only normal relative. Joanne often pitted the two brothers against each other. She would fight with Gavin, then cry to Jason to support her. She stood by while her sons came to blows over her, relishing Jason's attention.

Once Jason and I became engaged, Joanne treated me as if she were a jilted ex-lover. She meddled and provoked arguments between us. She gave me the cold shoulder at my bridal shower and interacted only with her table of guests. She glared at me during my mom's toast and sat with her arms folded whenever the attention was on me. She didn't give me a gift.

Despite the fact that my mom did not want me marrying Jason, she and I thoroughly enjoyed planning the wedding together. I hoped the shared enthusiasm would bring us closer and heal my family. I know she wanted that too. We particularly bonded over our animosity toward Joanne. We both agreed she was a manipulative troublemaker. My parents were paying for the wedding, so we got away with excluding Joanne from most of the plans. But I faced a dilemma when it came to shopping for my wedding dress. I didn't want Joanne there, and I knew my mom would feel slighted if I invited Joanne. But I also feared that if I didn't ask her along, she'd complain to Jason. I decided not to invite Joanne. Sure enough, she cried to Jason, who came to her defense and berated me.

Nothing seemed to flow easily. I was constantly strategizing and maneuvering around others because I wasn't centered in myself. I wasn't willing to acknowledge there were much bigger issues than who to invite dress shopping. I stayed in the confines of the crazy I knew, and somehow made it all the way to my wedding day.

~

On July 19, 1997 I sprang from my bed and looked out the window at the warm summer sunshine. It was a beautiful day for a wedding—finally my day to shine. Getting married was a huge accomplishment in my family, the ultimate goal and symbol of success. I wanted everyone to be proud of me. I wanted so much to belong. I was tired of wondering what was wrong with me, and of the loneliness that came from knowing I was wired differently. I couldn't wait to get ready.

I showered and drove to the salon for my hair and makeup appointment. For the last year and a half, I had planned every detail of my big day, including making sure to wear a button-down shirt to the salon so as not to ruin my updo. My mom had an appointment at the same salon, but we drove in separate cars so she could hurry back home and set up finger foods and champagne for the pre-church party. (Only Italians bombard the bride's house for appetizers before mass.)

I made my way back home from the salon in a full face of makeup, a headpiece adorning my curls. It was time to put on the dress. I felt like I was stepping into a clown suit. I weighed 120 pounds, and I think the dress—a sweetheart-top, trumpet-shaped gown with sheer sleeves and a sheer neckline covered in beads—weighed more.

I put on my wedding shoes and walked down the staircase of my childhood home. Like a member of some cult, I'd been brainwashed and draped in ceremonial clothes. The first person I saw in the living room was my best friend from college, Contessa. Her ice-blue eyes and extraordinary beauty stood out in spite of the factory-ordered bridesmaid dress and '90s updo. We'd had loads of fun together and made tons of wild memories over the years. Yet, I didn't confide in her about Jason or share my doubts about marrying him. She would have talked me out of it, and I wasn't ready to face the truth. She too came from a strong Italian background and learned you didn't meddle in other people's lives. If she had an opinion about my relationship with Jason or our over-the-top wedding, she kept it to herself. We locked eyes, and I sensed her confusion. She didn't recognize this version of me. I had let her down. I returned her uncertain smile, and we each grabbed a flute of champagne.

The house quickly filled with the rest of the bridesmaids and nosy relatives while the photographer captured the circus. My pulse raced. It was all happening so fast. Before I knew it, we were heading to church.

~

I stared out the window of the Rolls Royce I shared with Dad, searching for signs of Chuck. I made a deal with myself that if I noticed him standing on a corner or spying from his car, I would make a run for it. I needed an excuse to justify calling off the wedding, so I wouldn't have to take responsibility for the decision. I daydreamed that Chuck was standing in the distance, holding a bouquet of flowers, beckoning me to run away with him. He looked so handsome and adorable. I melted at his smile. Tears came to my eyes as I pictured myself running to him while I tore the veil from my head. But all I saw was the gas station and 7-Eleven across from the church and the pizza place on the corner. Chuck wasn't there. He did not indulge my immature fantasy of escape. He loved me, but he was done with me.

I wasn't brave enough to call off the wedding and risk being alone on an unknown path. I feared my instincts were reckless, so I silenced my soulful desires. A lifetime of doing that left me agitated and empty. I was sick of thinking something was wrong with me. Today would be the reset I needed. I convinced myself that the restless me would disappear if I could just embrace a conventional life. I stepped out of the limo while the photographer snapped away.

I entered the vestibule, where my eight bridesmaids stood alongside eight groomsmen in black rental tuxedos. My head spun. When I finally focused again, I saw Jason's mother. Joanne looked like a corpse in a black, skintight gown. She was Morticia Addams—actually, Broom Hilda. The days of skintight dresses were behind Joanne. She was too short to be elegant, and menopause had left her with flabby arms, a rounded belly, and wide hips. Her overdyed black hair hung to her butt. She'd drawn heavy black eyeliner around her eyes like a raccoon, and dark-brown lip liner way outside her lips. No lipstick—just liner. She stared at me with a wicked smile, then strutted down the aisle to her pew as if she were the one getting married.

The organ chimed, "Here Comes the Bride," and my father and I started toward the altar. The pews were packed with people looking at me, judging my dress, my hair, my makeup, *me*. I smiled, hoping they approved more than disapproved, not so much for myself but for my mother. I didn't think about Jason or the fact that I was about to get married. Desperate for approval, acceptance, and love, I was wondering if I was going to win the blue ribbon.

When we reached the front of the church, my father lifted my veil and kissed my cheek before nodding at Jason. He took his seat next to my mother as we all continued with the show. We had invested too much already to give it up.

The service was officiated by my childhood pastor. The familiar rituals and prayers were comforting. I knew my place, and I was determined to keep my life in order. A relative read a New Testament passage about love from the podium: "Love is patient, love is kind. It does not envy, it does not boast, it is not proud. It is not rude, it is not self-seeking, it is not easily angered, it keeps no record of wrongs. Love does not delight in evil but rejoices with the truth."

My stomach burned up to my throat. I was defying the Bible. I anticipated thunder and darkness would overtake the sky, but the sun shone through the stained-glass windows as Jason and I exchanged our vows. Suddenly, the church setting haunted me. I spotted the crucifix from the corner of my eye and became overcome by the gravity and finality of my promises.

The priest spoke his famous lines: "I now pronounce you man and wife. You may kiss the bride."

My fate was sealed.

~

We marched out of the church while the organ chimed a celebratory song. The congregation was giddy with cheer. Jason and I got into the Rolls Royce I had shared with my father earlier.

"You look fantastic," Jason said, pleased with me. My skin crawled. I felt like a mail order bride. I changed the subject and rambled on about how the weather was perfect for an outdoor cocktail party on the Prospect Isle Sound.

I felt nothing for Jason. I did what my family always did: ignored reality and pretended everything was okay by focusing on the external "good time." The little girl I had been at the dining room table at Sunday dinners, aware that something wasn't right, was long gone. As the bride, I was all in with the facade. I was turned off by this version of myself, but I brushed aside my disgust, the power of learned behavior far stronger than inner knowledge.

The reggae band, tiki bar, white sand, and palm trees at the cocktail hour were a welcome relief from the tense family photos and contrived couple shots. Our guests swooned with pleasure, and my parents and I shared a rare moment of satisfaction. My mother and I exchanged an amused glance over my mother-in-law, who had changed into a champagne-colored dress with an ornate wrap over her shoulders.

We made our way indoors for the reception. The band introduced the groom's parents, and Joanne entered, preening in all her glory. The wrap was gone, revealing her saggy, wrinkled cleavage. When my parents were introduced, they entered enthusiastically, my father pumping his fist in the air, excited for the party to start. We were really good at the pageantry. There was a long introduction of the bridal party, each pair walking in with a unique dance move.

Finally, Jason and I were introduced for the first time as Mr. and Mrs. Axcel. We walked in to rowdy and thunderous applause and took the dance floor for our first dance as husband and wife. The band solemnly played "All I Ask of You" from *Phantom of the Opera*. (I didn't realize until twenty years later that it was really a love song between Chuck and me. When I told Contessa about my revelation, she replied, "I always thought it was an odd choice.")

The energy of the band and the guests kept me on a high for a while. We eventually sat down to eat, and I gazed out from the bridal table, surveying my success. The centerpieces, the band, the food, the view, and the weather had turned out magnificently. My brothers and Jason were all on their best behavior. But my adrenaline high faded as the clock approached midnight. Soon, there would be nothing to distract me from reality. The plates were cleared, and the band took the stage once again. I downed champagne and embraced the couple of hours I had left.

The "highlight" of the party, the moment I kept rewinding on the wedding video but also couldn't bear to look at, was the mother–son dance. Jason escorted his mom to the center of the dance floor. Joanne pressed up against him, and they locked eyes for a moment before she laid her head on his shoulder. Her lips were slightly parted as she whispered something in his ear. He embraced her tenderly, and they moved together like lovers. For a surreal, frantic moment I wondered if they were going to start making out. Some of the guests exchanged sideways glances, as if asking, "Do you see what I'm seeing?" It became too uncomfortable to acknowledge, so we looked away. We all pretended we hadn't witnessed their blatant display as we moved on to the cake-cutting ceremony and Italian Venetian hour, a lavish display of every dessert item imaginable. We lost ourselves in cannoli and tiramisu, trying to unsee what we'd just seen.

~

Soon, guests began to say their goodbyes. Typically, Italians hand you an envelope of cash as they leave, but someone had decided that ritual was tacky. Instead, we had an equally tacky tulle-covered mailbox near the bridal table for guests to slip their envelopes in. My grandmother guarded that mailbox with her life while I kissed people on both cheeks.

"Congratulations!" said my cousin Jackie.

"Such a beautiful wedding!" exclaimed Jason's aunt.

"You looked beautiful!" my mom's best friend said.

My dad's friend Jimmy, an uncle to me, approached somberly and said, "Frannie, it's time to go." He winked and nodded toward my mother-in-law, adding, "She's melting!" in his best Wicked Witch of the West voice.

Random moments of connection and love can sustain us in

our darkest times. The last of the guests left, and I sat slumped on a wooden bench outside the catering hall, waiting for Jason and two of his groomsmen to finish their cigars. The party was over. My dress was rumpled, the train filthy from the dance floor. I held my shoes in my hand. I worried about what came next, but it wasn't the old-fashioned worry of a virgin bride about to consummate her marriage. We'd already been physically intimate over the years. I tolerated the obligation and had grown used to the vague sense of violation and cheapness I felt afterward. What scared me was the magnitude of being Jason's wife.

I wanted to hide my despair but was growing more desperate by the moment. Tracy and Fiona, the girlfriends of the groomsmen Jason was smoking with, came over. I made room for them to sit with me. The warm July night air smelled like childhood summers, but carefree days were a distant memory now. Young Francesca was gone. Tracy and Fiona sat with me the way you would sit with someone in mourning. We had gotten to know each other well over the past few years. They didn't have to say much; I felt their presence. They knew I would suffer, but they also knew I would survive. Or maybe that's what I knew, and their kind eyes reflected it. I believe they would have sat with me forever if they could have. They were good people with loving souls. They looked at me, not through me. The warmth in their eyes said they liked what they saw. My chest swelled, and my eyes teared up. It felt so good to be seen. That moment offered me a strength that I would soon desperately need.

chapter five

I WOKE UP IN A BED-AND-BREAKFAST OVERLOOKING MISTY
Gray Harbor, NY, my body heavy with dread. It was my first day as
a newlywed, and I had to go to my in-laws' for brunch with Jason's
family and friends. My arms stiffened, and my chest tightened. I
resented being at the mercy of everyone else's agenda. My parents
had been half-heartedly invited two days before the wedding, but
none of my other relatives or friends were asked.

I pulled myself together in the bathroom, but my youthful
glow was tinged with sadness. An imposter stared back at me in
the mirror. It would be many years before I would see my true
self again. Jason seemed oblivious to, or unaffected by, my sadness. He was eager to get to his mother's and smoke cigars with
his fraternity brothers. I was simply the trophy wife.

Joanne and her husband, Paulie, lived in what was once a
maid's cottage on a large piece of property in an exclusive neighborhood. The roads wound majestically, and behind stately trees
stood the grand homes of wealthy Majestic Mile residents.
Joanne thought this made her American royalty, but her driveway
had potholes and was surrounded by a brown lawn covered in
dog poop. At the edge of the driveway stood her tiny white house,
listing to one side slightly, in desperate need of renovations they
couldn't afford.

Joanne had met Paulie, a Wall Street big shot, while he was

married to someone else. Paulie eventually divorced his wife and married Joanne. They lived a wealthy lifestyle for a few years until the Feds came in and seized their assets because Paulie wasn't paying his taxes. Joanne desperately tried to live among the wealthy, even when the money was gone. She believed gold hoop earrings, old fur coats, and a certain zip code maintained her status.

When we arrived at the brunch, Joanne was gloating like a queen, a satisfied smile plastered to her face. My mother hunched on a folding chair on the brown lawn. This was not the elegant garden party she'd imagined. The eggs were runny, the croissants were stale, and the champagne was cheap. Mom always had high hopes for me. I had let her down. Her disappointment cut me to the core. Her desolate gaze confirmed my deep fear: I had amounted to nothing more than ordinary.

I stood alone in the middle of the party tent, a plastic champagne flute in my hand. My heels sank in the dirt while the inane chatter of Joanne's forty party guests hummed in my ears. I felt myself dim, as if a glow within me went out. It had been fading for years. I recalled the moments when I felt the flicker of desire but hadn't been brave enough to fan the flames.

I had declared the wrong major, accepted jobs I didn't care about, and lived with my parents instead of getting a city apartment after I graduated college. I'd participated in social activities that didn't interest me and stayed in relationships that didn't feel right. I can't say I wasn't warned; I'd felt a twinge of guilt each time. I thought if I excelled at the status quo, I would overcome my self-betrayal. Instead, I had faded to nothing. Suddenly, nothing mattered. Disorienting grief set in. I could no longer remember my dreams, but I knew I wasn't living them. They became pangs of longing that plagued me for most of my adult life.

Jason's cousin walked up to me and said something nice about the wedding. I shook off my angst. I was married. The wedding was spectacular. I had a very nice life ahead of me. There would be a house and children for me to take care of one day. I just had to smile and enjoy what I could.

~

After the brunch, we drove to my parents' to pick up my belongings. I stood on the threshold of my childhood room and gazed at the spring break pictures and sorority letters on the wall. A picture of me and my brothers sat on my dresser. We were young and smiling, our arms around each other, drinks in our hands. My trophies and awards filled the room, along with other mementos of what had once seemed like an accomplished life.

I remembered the times I hid in my room reading for hours as a child, and later, as a teen, talking endlessly on my phone. My stuffed Snoopy doll from Chuck was on the bed. I yearned to take it with me. I missed the girl who once lived in this room, the one who got so lost along the way. I brushed a tear from my cheek as I wondered if I'd ever see her again. Sensing my pain was bubbling too strong, I took a deep breath and hurriedly gathered my bags, convincing myself these were normal emotions to have as I said goodbye to my childhood.

Suitcases in hand, I met my parents at the bottom of the stairs. My father faded from my focus. My mom's fearful face and sad eyes were all I could see. She didn't know what to say; she never did. But I could tell she realized the way she and my father lived had set me up for an even worse fate.

There had been times when Jason and I stopped dating. My mom had been hopeful during the breaks. She grew angry when we got back together. "What's wrong with you, Francesca? Can you be this stupid to take this jerk back again?" she'd scolded.

Her disgust triggered me. "You should talk," I snapped back. "Where do you think I learned this crap from?" I was alluding to her taking my dad back after they separated briefly when I was in high school.

In the past, she'd lashed out. Today, she grieved. Her sorrow unleashed my suffering. Her blue eyes appeared a dull gray, the outer corners turned down. Her frown hung down to her chin. She regretted being unable to stop the cycle. Her shoulders slumped. Watching your child suffer is worse than suffering yourself. I was scared. I wanted my mother to take care of me and make my marriage go away. We stared at each other, aware that we had both made terrible mistakes. I choked back a blubbering cry of despair.

Jason walked into the hallway from the living room, and I felt him looking at me with warning eyes and a tight jaw. He sensed the high emotions and was eager to get out of there and have me all to himself. He swung his arms and subtly punched a fist into his palm. His lack of patience and hate for my parents was obvious. He sensed my emotional pull toward my family, even though they were dysfunctional. I had too much guilt to walk away and a heart that yearned to heal. He knew this would make it difficult for him to fully control and dominate me. He picked up my suitcases. "Let's go," he said. "It's time to say goodbye."

~

En route to our honeymoon in Hawaii, I moved forward in high-functioning anxiety mode. I called ahead to confirm reservations, repeatedly checked for plane tickets in my bag, and studied the itinerary I'd written out on a legal pad. The more I tried to control my jumpy nerves, the stronger the need to control my life. Jason was happy to have me be such a doer. He had no inclination to take care of things that didn't matter to him. He got away with being lazy by saying that my take-charge ambition was cute. Most people assumed this was just my personality. Jason was keen enough to know it was fueled by my fear.

I was on a mission to enjoy Hawaii and be stronger than my volatile emotions. I tried to lose myself in the beauty of the islands, willing away my negative feelings toward my husband.

Jason, on the other hand, was over-the-top with exaggerated enthusiasm. "This is my *wife*," he said proudly, introducing me at the front desk of the resort. I smiled like a dope. Memories from the Disney resort haunted me.

"Can I get my lovely *wife* a drink?" he asked poolside. I hid behind my sunglasses, pretending to read a magazine. I couldn't bring myself to play along. I recalled the limo driver from the night we got engaged, how he'd seen right through me.

"Reservation for *Mr. and Mrs.* Axcel," he later emphasized to the hostess at the restaurant. I fussed with my purse. I was embarrassed for him. His manner was so rehearsed and insincere, he made me cringe. I'd seen him play this character many times since our first date.

Even on my honeymoon, I felt drained by how much effort our marriage took. I was exhausted from pretending to be fine when I wasn't. But I was determined to make us a normal couple. We had candlelit dinners, took walks on the beach, and drank champagne. But the attempts at romance only deepened my sense of emptiness. Everywhere I looked, I spied other couples who seemed genuinely in love. We took a helicopter ride with one couple, and a bike ride down a volcano with several others. I coped better in group activities, but loneliness ran through my veins when I recognized real joy in others that I could not feel. They held hands with ease, sat on hammocks with their arms and legs intertwined, and made sincere eye contact when they spoke to each other. My insides hollowed. I longed for connection, attraction, and love, the things I'd had with Chuck. I wished I was in Hawaii with him.

Jason and I returned to our room between daytime activities and dinner, each of us resting from the facade in our own way. He plopped on the bed in his boxer shorts, watched sports, and ate chips. He cradled one stubby leg over the other and picked at the skin on his feet. His general lack of etiquette repulsed me. I wasn't attracted to his squat build or his personality. His beady eyes were too close together, his usual expression dubious. I had such an aversion for Jason that I did not realize it masked profound self-hatred. It would be many years before I let those demons out.

I called my mom. "What's new at home?" I asked.

"Not much," she replied. "How's Hawaii?" She didn't use the word honeymoon, nor did she ask how Jason was doing.

"The resort is nice," I blandly replied. "Have you heard from anyone about the wedding?" I asked, eager to hear what people had thought about it. I'd identified with the wedding for so long that I didn't know what else to think about.

"Yes, people have been calling. Everyone had a great time. They're all saying what a beautiful wedding it was."

"Did you get any pictures back yet?" I asked.

"Just a few from Mrs. Russo. It was nice of her to take some." Mrs. Russo was Mom's best friend. "I'm sure the proofs from the photographer will be ready soon," she added.

"What did people say about my dress?" I asked, trying to keep the distraction of the wedding alive.

"Everyone said you looked beautiful."

After several days of these calls, my mother must have realized I was trying to fill a void. She limited her responses and did not indulge my wedding recap talk. I was holding onto the wedding because the honeymoon wasn't cutting it for me. Mom's dismissiveness seemed like her way of telling me to accept my situation, carry on, and try to live happily. She must have been nervous I would crack. I feared she would not support my unraveling. I was alone in my anguish.

chapter six

WE RETURNED FROM OUR HONEYMOON, AND IT HIT ME THAT I wasn't going home. Jason and I had leased an apartment in Bay Terrace, Queens, and had furniture delivered a couple of weeks before the wedding. I'd spent a Sunday unpacking shower gifts with my mom, like a little girl setting up a dollhouse. But I hadn't really thought about moving in. The car service dropped us off, and my mind went numb as my body unpacked. I noticed Mom had stocked the fridge while we were gone, and the loving gesture brought tears to my eyes.

The next morning, I boarded the express bus to Manhattan. The unfamiliar commute to work made me feel even more alone in the world. I settled in at my cubicle, shared some pictures, and gave a positive recap of the wedding day. I played the part of happy newlywed, adding how beautiful Hawaii was. Keeping up pretenses exhausted me. I couldn't wait for five o'clock.

Later that evening, I walked back up the path to our garden apartment, my feet throbbing in my heels. I grabbed the mail from our mailbox and opened the door to our first-floor unit. Jason was slouched on the couch, watching TV. My eyes narrowed in disgust. "Hi!" I said. I summoned the effort and tried to make the best of it, hoping to keep my growing despair at bay.

"What's up?" He barely looked up from the TV.

"Not much. Just let me change, and then I guess I'll get dinner started." He didn't offer to help.

I went into our bedroom and found the bed unmade. I resented having to leave for work before Jason was even awake. His towel was on the bathroom floor. I angrily picked it up. *He thinks he's so handsome; he likes acting all dapper in his suits. Little do people know what a slob he really is.* I stewed while I changed out of my work clothes, straightened the bed, and headed toward the kitchen.

"I was thinking chicken cutlets, rice, and a salad?" I asked.

"Sure," he said, but he wasn't really paying attention.

The phone rang. Jason didn't move.

"Hello?" I answered.

"Is Jason Paul there?" Ugh, Joanne. I hadn't spoken to her since the brunch.

"It's your mom." I handed him the phone.

He sat up. "Hi, gorgeous!" he exclaimed. I rolled my eyes as I turned back toward the kitchen. I prepared dinner while they chatted. I had a few choice words for both of them running in my head. It was easier to attack them than hold myself accountable for the poor choices I had made.

My emotions could get so intense, I feared they would overwhelm me. As resentment and rage bubbled, I distracted myself by setting the table with the pretty new dishes and glasses we'd received for our wedding. I lit dinner candles and put out cloth napkins in sunflower napkin rings while trying to shelve my anger.

"Dinner's ready!" I yelled. Jason blew kisses to his mother over the phone.

He sat down at the table and started to eat. "Not a bad first attempt," he said mockingly after he swallowed a forkful of chicken and rice. "You'll get used to the cooking thing." I tried to laugh, pretending he was just being playful, even though his tone told me otherwise.

"The express bus was horrible," I shared as I pushed my food around my plate. "It took over ninety minutes and was stop-and-go the whole time."

"That's too bad." He shrugged, signaling that it wasn't his problem.

"Someone at my office suggested I take the Prospect Isle Railroad between Penn Station and Bay Terrace. The train only takes thirty-five minutes. But the station's about two miles from the apartment." We had one car, and Jason used it to drive to work at a solo practitioner's office on Prospect Isle. "I was thinking maybe you could drive me to the station in the morning and pick me up at night," I prompted when he didn't reply.

Jason pursed his lips. "I can't drive you in the morning. I don't have to leave that early, and it's in the opposite direction. And I don't want to worry about having to leave the office to pick you up from the train in the evening. What if Tom needs me to stick around?" Suddenly he was acting responsible.

"I guess I can walk." I was annoyed that he was trying to bullshit me, and I resented his authority over the car. I kept it to myself. If I opened my mouth, I would unleash my pent-up rage. I had to get myself under control.

Jason was lazy in his career and even lazier at home. According to him, taking care of the house was "women's work." He didn't care what the apartment looked like; if I wanted it clean, I had to clean it myself. I scrubbed the bathroom and kitchen while he watched sports. I had to vacuum when he wasn't busy talking to his mom on the phone. I did the grocery shopping and planned meals for the week. On Saturday mornings, Jason used the car to meet his dad for breakfast, a ritual they shared on and off over the years whenever they were on speaking terms. The local laundromat was several blocks from our apartment. I had to walk, my arms shaking from the weight of the baskets. My ego couldn't handle failure. I would hold everything together if it killed me. But married life was depleting me. I was thin as a rail, had dark circles under my eyes, and had dry, damaged hair.

I cleaned up the dinner dishes while Jason smoked a cigar on the front steps. I wondered what I needed him in my life for, and worse, why I allowed him to call the shots. I did all the chores, *and* I was the main breadwinner. What was he contributing to our marriage? Anger burned through me as I scrubbed the dishes hard. The worst part: I had known all this before I married him.

We'd lost out on the first apartment we applied for because Jason's income wasn't sufficient to cover his law school debt. My parents tried to caution me by pointing out I was debt-free, thanks to them. I was determined to prove we would be just fine, holding on to the image of us as blooming professionals. When we found a replacement apartment, I filled out the application as an individual so it would be approved.

After the wedding, I'd planned to deposit the monetary gifts we received in the bank. I had a personal account; Jason shared one with his mom. He insisted we open a joint account, because he did not want all the wedding money in my name only. It was one of the few Saturday errands he ran with me. From that day forward, our paychecks went to the joint account, mine nearly twice as much as his. Assets were joint; liabilities were mine.

The next morning, I walked to the train station through one of my favorite sections of Bay Terrace. The streets were lined with old oak trees and Tudor-style homes. Chuck lived nearby, and I lost myself in sweet memories of him and of my younger years. Closer to the station, I passed his gym, bars where we once hung out, and the busy strip where I had spent so many nights out with friends. The memories intensified. The longing for Chuck and my old life came up so strongly, I could no longer bottle the grief. I tucked myself in a window seat on the train, put my head against the glass, and cried all the way into Manhattan. I dried my eyes and blew my nose in a Penn Station bathroom before walking over to my office.

For months, I commuted to and from work in tears, head on the window, painfully longing for the life I didn't choose. Strangers eyed me sympathetically, minding their business while I let it all out. I worked so hard to bottle up my pain and keep up appearances in my circle. It was such a relief to be anonymous, lost in a sea of busy New York commuters, unloading my burden without constraint.

Every night at the end of my commute home, I took a deep breath and summoned the strength to put my key into our front door lock. Over the months we'd been living together, I'd come up against several versions of Jason. I couldn't predict which one I'd find waiting for me. Sometimes he ignored me. Other times, he verbally abused me, and occasionally, he used physical force. Often, his rage was fueled by his mother.

One night, he sat at the head of our table and angrily chewed his dinner, his utensils scraping his plate. I had no idea what had sparked his anger, but it didn't matter. He was going to take it out on me.

"What's the matter?" I finally asked when I couldn't stand the icy silence anymore.

"I'll tell you what's the matter." He pointed his fork at me. "You're a disrespectful bitch."

"What are you talking about?" My tone was a mix of irritation and fear.

"My mother called crying today. She said you were rude to her yesterday on Mother's Day."

"What the hell did I do now?" My fork clattered onto my plate. I wasn't in the mood to put up with his nonsense. We'd spent most of Mother's Day at Joanne's and had only stopped by to see my mom for coffee in the evening. Every holiday played out that way—we spent most of our time at Joanne's. Jason gleefully laughed in his mom's kitchen, planted kisses on her forehead, and joked with his cousins as we sat around a folding table in her tiny space. Dog hair was everywhere, and the smell of damp dogs filled the air. I missed my mom's cooking and her bustling dining room, where I knew my brothers, aunts and uncles, and cousins were having one of the boisterous family gatherings we always had. I longed for the comfort of the familiar setting I had once tried to escape. When we finally arrived for a late cameo appearance at my parents', Jason sat scowling, looking at his watch, and giving me the "let's go" eye. I spent the little time I had with my family trying to keep the peace.

"You cleared the table but didn't clear her dish," Jason said as if he were accusing me of a crime.

I'd been putting up with their twisted relationship, her jealousy and manipulation, and his infatuation with her, since we got engaged. After almost three years, I'd had it.

"This is what she does?" I shot back. "Calls you to make trouble with her made-up bullshit? She's mental, and so are you." Part of me loved a good fight. It gave me a place to take out all my anger. It felt good to blame Jason and Joanne for my unhappiness.

Jason pushed his chair back from the table and stood up, knocking a dish to the floor. He glowered down at me and grabbed my hair. "You don't want to clear my mother's plate? Now you're gonna clean up the floor." He pushed my head forward toward the shattered plate.

I'd wanted to leave him since the honeymoon, but I refused to give my family the satisfaction that they'd been right—that I was a fool. Dealing with his abuse seemed easier than dealing with failure. My stubborn will was stronger than his wrath. I refused to let him and his mother's sick behavior get the best of me.

~

We lived a dark existence behind closed doors but had a bubbly social life with our friends. Going to parties and bars with other couples offered me temporary relief from my marriage. I was so emotionally far gone, intermittent moments of fun were enough to convince me that my marriage wasn't so bad. Delusion and alcohol even allowed some physical intimacy to exist. I could tolerate sex with him after a couple of drinks.

Jason liked spending time smoking cigars, watching sports, and playing cards with his fraternity brothers. I used that time to sneak in a visit to my family or go shopping with my mom. I tried to live around my husband, but no matter what I did, his wrath caught up with me. One weekend, I got my eyebrows waxed at a salon. The wax burned my skin, leaving what looked like a bruise above my left eye.

"What the hell happened to you?" Jason asked when he got home.

"I had my eyebrows waxed, and the woman burned me."

"Let me see that," he barked. He stormed right up into my face.

"Who did this to you?" he demanded.

I was taken aback by his fury. "What are you talking about? The lady at the nail salon," I reiterated.

He leaned into me. "Don't lie to me. Did one of your brothers hit you when you visited your mother today?" He was ready for a fight.

"What the hell are you talking about? Of course not!" There was no basis whatsoever for his accusation.

"If I ever find out they hit you, I'll break their arms." He glared at me another moment and then stormed away.

Jason was so confident in his conviction that I wondered if it was reasonable to assume I had been hit. He genuinely believed his interpretation of reality, so much so he distorted mine. I started to think maybe I didn't see things for how they really were. Maybe he wasn't so abusive; maybe I was the problem. Perhaps his mother was a kind woman, and I was the nasty one. Maybe our marriage wasn't as bad as I made it out to be. I grew so disoriented, I wondered if I was the unstable one. I had always ignored my inner voice, even when I heard it clearly. By now I couldn't trust it; I couldn't even discern it. I started to hang back and let life happen to me.

The weeks turned into months. I got a break on the nights Jason watched a Yankees game or *The Simpsons*. I'd get in our car and drive around aimlessly, relishing the temporary peace and freedom. My mind wandered as I drove. Sometimes I went as far as my old neighborhood, where I dropped in to see my mom, pretending everything was okay as we shared a cup of tea. There was no way I fooled her; she was way too astute. I felt temporary peace after those visits, like she was a sponge that soaked up all my unspoken pain.

Other nights I found myself driving dangerously close to Chuck's house, until the night I was bold enough to park out front. His car was parked at its usual spot along the curb, adding to my delusion that we could pick up where we'd left off. I clutched the steering wheel and played out our reunion in my mind.

"I screwed up," I would say when he answered the door. "I love you. I've always loved you," I would add. Chuck would take me by the hand into the house and hold me in his arms. We would begin anew. But I couldn't get out of my car. I was too afraid he would reject me. I wasn't ready to let the fantasy end. My daydreams were all I had left.

I parked outside Chuck's house on countless nights during my first year of marriage. Playing out our romantic reunion kept me going, until the gut-wrenching night I saw Chuck's girlfriend get out of her car. My stomach flipped, and I gasped. She walked into his house through the side kitchen door as I'd done count-less times. I was a fool to think he was waiting for me. I sobbed, head on the steering wheel, snot running from my nose until there was nothing left in me. I don't know if it was Chuck I longed for or my lost self.

I drove home and slipped into the apartment like I was hid-ing an affair. I was so ashamed of myself, I figured Jason was as good a husband as I deserved. My dreams of a better life seemed like childish fantasies. Once again, I decided to make the best of the marriage. After all, there seemed no turning back.

～

I booked a trip to London and Paris for our first wedding an-niversary. Jason called his mom from the hotel room in London.

"Jason Paul! Is that you?" I heard her shriek through the receiver.

"It is, Mom." He smiled, his tone thick with adoration. Anger bubbled inside me. He worshipped his mother, even though she was a troublemaker. My mother received no recognition. Mom had recently offered to let me drop our laundry off at her house. It bothered her that I was schlepping baskets to and from the laundromat. She returned folded loads in baskets while we were at work, leaving them in the entry hall so as not to intrude. Her latest delivery before our trip had included a shopping bag with a new outfit for me. Jason scowled when I told him about her gesture.

He finally ended his international call with his mom. He put his hand up to his heart and said to me, "Little Paulie is going to be a dad. Such beautiful news." He looked like an elderly man savoring special moments of younger family members.

"You don't even speak to him," I blurted. I couldn't stomach his phoniness. He despised his stepbrother.

"He's family!" he snapped.

"You don't respect my family," I shot back.

He grabbed me by my hair and dragged me across the room, opened the hotel door, and flung me into the hallway. I stumbled into the wall and then looked up and down the hall, unsure what to do. I had to get my things, or at least my shoes. I knocked on the door over and over until my knuckles hurt. A hotel employee eventually let me back into the room. Jason had ransacked my suitcase and thrown my things all over the floor. He'd ripped a sleeve off the new outfit my mom bought me and torn a gash down the front.

I put on shoes, grabbed my bag, and stormed out, my body

trembling from anger and shock. I walked the streets until my fury faded. As I calmed down, I realized I loved being alone in a foreign country where no one knew me and I had no one to answer to. The sudden burst of freedom was exhilarating. I spent the next couple of days touring London by myself. I strolled through Hyde Park, stood in awe at the Abbey, and gazed at Big Ben. I hadn't felt so alive in years.

I returned to the hotel room late each night. I had no idea how Jason spent his time, nor did I care. He didn't possess his usual bullying command over me. Eventually, the fight blew over, and we went back to pretending we were a normal couple on our way to Paris. But I felt out of place there. I wasn't sophisticated or interesting. I was an insecure victim of domestic abuse in a toxic marriage. A European vacation wasn't going to change that.

chapter seven

THE TRUTH ABOUT OUR ANNIVERSARY TRIP HAUNTED ME. I FELT like an accessory to a crime. When coworkers and family members asked about it, I talked about landmark attractions like a world traveler but made no mention of us as a couple. I wasn't brave enough to come clean. I continued to live around what was really happening.

My sister-in-law was hosting a surprise thirtieth birthday party for my older brother. I dreaded asking Jason if we could attend, so I conspicuously left the invitation on the kitchen counter. Then I waited for a night when he seemed to be in a good mood, laughing at an episode of *The Simpsons*.

"I'm going to respond yes to Heather about the surprise party," I said nonchalantly.

Jason kept his eyes on the television. The veins in his temples pulsed—not a good sign. I held my breath. He slowly turned his head and looked at me, his nostrils flaring and his lips pressed together. "Are you kidding me?"

All my strategizing about how and when to ask him had been a waste of energy. I sat next to him on the couch, desperate for a last-minute save. "Don't let my brother come between us." I tried to get my way by going along with his hatred for Dominick. I could tell by the tension in his face and the way he angrily turned toward me that he wasn't fooled. I took a breath and mentally checked out in anticipation of a venomous scolding.

Instead, my husband spit in my face. My mind went numb with disbelief. I raised my hand to my cheek, stunned. My fingers came away wet. I stared at Jason blankly, unable to grasp what he'd done.

"I'm not going. And I tell you what, you're not going either. Understood?" he warned. I wasn't capable of walking out on him, and he knew it. Recognizing my weakness, he relaxed back into the couch and smirked.

I went to bed, where I stared at the ceiling trying to envision how it would play out if I divorced him. Glimpses of freedom and strength were overshadowed by anticipated judgment of others. I could hear the gossip ringing in my ears: *Divorced after one year? I thought she was so smart—what a mess! I guess her fancy degree and her lawyer husband weren't so special after all. Now what is she going to do?* I felt the weight of disappointment from my mom and the nakedness of personal shame. I dreaded being exposed as a fraud more than I dreaded Jason's abuse. I refused to allow my brokenness to surface. Every time my toxic marriage got worse, I became more determined to fix it. I just had to get better at avoiding his triggers. I tried to make a mental list of the situations that set him off, but the list was long and evolving. All I could do was try to keep one step ahead of him.

I began to look for a starter house in the suburbs, the next expected step after marriage, before kids. Moving to Prospect Isle was a natural progression from Queens. Jason chose a neighborhood in the town of Rocky Bluff. He convinced me he needed to establish residency there because it was required by his Republican Club. He saw a path to a role for himself in local politics. What seemed like career aspirations was nothing more than manipulation to set himself up for an easy no-show job. I didn't give it much thought. My world was so small, I never even thought to live anywhere else. No one from my background moved away from Queens or Prospect Isle. If they did, they were outcasts.

I did most of the house hunting on my own. I spent weekend after weekend looking at listings with agents. I found the cutest little gingerbread house, which worked very well in my make-believe life. Jason approved. It was affordable and was located where he wanted to be. My mom approved because it showed I could afford a house, plus her godson had already moved to the same town, so I was keeping in line with our extended family.

My mom and I scrubbed the kitchen and bathroom, picked out paint colors, and planted flowers in the garden. We washed the windows, set up the furniture, and decorated the living room. My parents bought us a patio set and grill. We had to make a show of the house the way we made a show of the wedding. Jason took advantage of all our labor and all the other perks he got out of the experience. We used wedding gifts plus my bonuses as a deposit. His office handled the closing. Everything was taken care of for him.

In what felt like an ongoing power struggle between our families, Joanne made her presence known at our new home. I shook my head in disbelief when she rang our doorbell on Sunday mornings with bagels and coffee for two. She and Jason sat at the kitchen table my grandmother had purchased for us and chatted, sometimes with his hand over hers. I made my own coffee and busied myself around the house.

Underlying sadness and the feeling like something was missing in my life crept through me. The new house wasn't enough. The high wore off as quickly as the wedding. I began daydreaming about having a baby and becoming a mom. I anticipated feeling a sense of purpose that would finally bring me joy. I longed for deep connections and the love I imagined the baby would bring into my world. Not so much with Jason, but with my family and myself. When I looked at the positive pregnancy test the summer of 1999, I thought, *yes; this will make life complete.*

An exciting yet eerie energy stirred toward the end of that year and the start of the new century. People were expecting some Y2K disaster and havoc. Joanne forbade my brother-in-law Gavin from going to Times Square with friends for New Year's Eve. At the time, he lived with her and Paulie, even though he was twenty-nine years old. He'd taken some time off between college and law school, so he was a recent law school graduate. Gavin stayed home, lit the fireplace, and drank alone while Joanne and Paulie were out. Jason and I went to a couple of house parties in Queens. I was our designated driver, because I was six months pregnant. We made our way back home well after midnight and went to bed. I was exhausted from the pregnancy, and Jason seemed drained from a night of alcohol and cigars. But something seemed off. I could sense he was lying awake.

Suddenly, Jason shot up, gasped for air, and pounded on his chest. "I can't breathe! I can't breathe!" He panicked. If we were older, I would have thought he was having a heart attack. His eyes seemed fixed on something distant, as if he were seeing something that wasn't there. I was alarmed but tried to stay calm.

"Just calm down!" I commanded. "Maybe you had too much to drink tonight." My yelling seemed to bring his focus back to our bedroom. His breathing slowly returned to normal, and we went to sleep.

Later that night, I felt a tug on my arm. "Gavin?" I looked up, confused. My brother-in-law was standing next to my bed wearing a tuxedo. "Gavin, what are you doing here?" I asked. He tipped a champagne glass toward my belly as if to toast the baby. I woke from the dream to the ringing of our phone.

"Hello?" Jason anxiously answered. He listened for a few moments, then said, "Oh my God! I'm on my way!" He threw a flannel over his T-shirt, pulled on jeans, and slid into sneakers. "I'm going to my mom's. Stay here," he commanded before he ran out the door.

There always seemed to be some sort of drama in our life, especially when it came to Joanne. She'd recently been taking advantage of insurance coverage to make necessary renovations to her cottage. After storms, she called the power company, demanding settlements for downed trees on her power lines. Recently her basement had flooded, and she hoped to collect enough to clean up the mess and then some. She scammed more than she worked. I suspected that maybe she had staged some sort of incident, hoping to file an insurance claim. It wasn't the most charitable thought, but I wouldn't have put it past her. I tried to go back to bed, but after a couple of hours I sensed something was very wrong. Finally, my phone rang.

"My brother's dead," Jason said, his tone flat.

"What?" I gasped.

"Car accident."

"Oh my God." I couldn't comprehend what was happening.

"Don't tell anyone," he said. "I'll be home soon."

I called my parents. They were horrified and wanted to come be with us. "Jason doesn't want anyone to know yet," I said. I hung up and began taking down Christmas decorations. Italians don't put out decorations when someone dies. Suddenly the lighted reindeer on my front lawn seemed disrespectful.

Jason pulled in the driveway, and I met him at our side kitchen door. I stared at him, not sure what to say or do. "Make up with your brothers," he righteously said as he charged past me and down to our basement. I followed him down the stairs but stopped dead in my tracks at the bottom. He was rolling around on the floor, sobbing like a wounded animal. His spasms frightened me. I had no idea what tragic grief looked like, but he seemed to be exaggerating. He peeked through one eye and caught me observing him, then carried on with his outburst. A jolt of energy flashed through me. I sensed his over-the-top show of emotions was meant to cover coldhearted emptiness. I knew in that instant that he was dangerous. He did not seek comfort, nor was I able to offer it.

Eventually he got up and brushed by me. I was reminded of the lack of connection between us as he went back up to the kitchen. He made call after call to his relatives and friends, repeating the news in the same exact tone. "My mom came home, and they had one of their arguments. She told him to get out. He grabbed the keys but was in no condition to drive. He hit a tree a mile from the house."

Jason spent the next few days setting up services and picking out a cemetery plot with his parents. He asked me to cut a check to cover the costs.

At the wake, Jason greeted guests like he was hosting a function. Relatives, friends, and local politicians attended. My parents came but not my brothers, ultimately giving Jason more ammunition. He shook each person's hand and patted them on the shoulder in the same exact manner. He said goodbye one by one, thanking each person for coming as if he had hosted a formal dinner party. I didn't know what to make of it. My mother and grandmother wept; their heartfelt grief was a stark contrast to Jason's political mannerisms. Their vulnerability made me feel less crazy.

There had only been one moment during the wake in which I saw a different look on Jason's face.

"Dana." He sounded touched, even though he acted as if he'd been expecting her. Dana was his college sweetheart. She had eventually married one of his fraternity brothers.

"I'm sorry for your loss," she said, glancing at her husband, then me.

Jason put his arms out wide, beckoning her to give him a big hug. I saw that familiar smirk on his face as she came into his embrace; he still had her under his thumb. Her husband stood stiffly to the side as Jason grinned at him over Dana's shoulder. The joy of anticipated revenge danced in his eyes.

~

The funeral mass was the next morning. "Happy Birthday, Ben!" Jason shook my dad's hand outside the church. I found that so odd. It's strange the things I remember from that day, such as Jason's ability to give a charismatic eulogy, or the eye contact I made with my mom and grandmother, who were crying in their pew as we processed out of church behind the coffin. They cried with grief and for what they knew would be a heavy load for me to bear. I still see flashes of moments etched in my mind, like when Joanne grabbed for the coffin, trying to open it before a pallbearer held her back. I was ashamed of myself for relating to her desperation, as if I had a familiar despair in my life.

After the cemetery, we went to lunch with a restaurant full of mourners, followed by a small gathering of close friends at our house. I sat in the living room with a few of Jason's friends, who expressed concern for his detached behavior throughout the services. They feared it was denial and that grief would hit hard in the days to come. Their awareness and their understanding of human emotions comforted me. Deep down, I knew Jason was wired differently than the rest of us. The next day, he went back to work. I thought it was too soon, but I followed his lead and returned to my office too.

My life seemed so out of whack, I became a nervous wreck. It was flooded with problems and now tragedies, while others seemed to live simply, peacefully. The constant churn of anxiety turned into contractions. I scheduled an appointment with my doctor, worried about the safety of the baby. But I think I just needed help in general. I was worried about how life was spinning, and I was desperate for someone to hold me steady. I feared how bad things might get. My need to control my circumstances grew stronger and stronger. My anxiety intensified as I feared I would lose control. I couldn't confide in friends; their lives seemed normal, so I had to pretend I was fine. I couldn't confide in my family; we didn't have meaningful conversations. I certainly couldn't confide in Jason. I didn't feel safe. Plus, he was never available.

Night after night, Jason went to visit his mom. Joanne moved into Paulie's apartment in a condo complex, known for divorcees, only a few minutes from our house. I didn't even know he had one. Apparently, he kept a rental over the years because they'd separated so often. Oftentimes, if Jason wasn't already there, Paulie called urgently needing his help when he found Joanne on the bathroom floor, pills scattered about her from suicide attempts. Her episodes led to frequent, brief stays in the psychiatric ward.

Paulie needed a break. Joanne started staying on our couch. Next thing I knew, I was very pregnant, still commuting to work, and living with Joanne.

I noticed a pattern in her behavior. In front of Jason and others, she was in a depressed trance. But alone in the house with me, she perked up. She enjoyed being waited on and became a fixture in my living room, watching TV and discussing shows. She had no boundaries and was very happily settling into my space. She actually seemed to be enjoying herself. But just as quickly as she came to life, she slipped into hopeless despair again whenever other people were around.

"The doctor called me," Jason said on the phone with his dad. "Her blood work indicates that she isn't taking the medication." I'm not sure what was said on the other end, but after a pause, Jason replied, "I just don't get it. He thinks she's pretending."

Not too long after that call, I was alone with Joanne in the house again. Jason was out for the evening with friends. I really had to use the bathroom, but Joanne was taking a shower. She finally came out with a towel on her head and walked by me as if she were at a spa. I used the bathroom and just wanted to relax, but I couldn't even sit in my own living room. She was sprawled out on the couch watching TV with her dog.

"You can't stay here once we have the baby," I blurted.

"Does it bother you that I'm here?" she asked provokingly.

"We just don't have the room, and it's going to get a lot more hectic here after the baby's born," I explained, sensing I'd fallen into a trap.

"I'll let Jason Paul know you asked me to leave," she warned.

It dawned on me that he wasn't around much. I wondered

what he was doing. He told me he was getting Joanne's affairs in order or helping Paulie find them a new place to live.

Years later, I learned the truth when I ran into Jenn, a friend from high school, at the beach. We hadn't seen each other in years. She happened to be married to one of Jason's fraternity brothers. Queens was an incestuous place. We stood at the edge of the water and caught up while the kids swam around.

"You look great," she cheerfully said. "I'm so happy things worked out for you."

"Yes," I agreed. "I'm happy. And well over that marriage." I rolled my eyes.

"I always thought he was such a jerk. My husband can't stand him either," she said. Then she added, "I couldn't believe he was sleeping with Dana while you were pregnant," as if I already knew.

"Two losers," I said, playing along, but I was stunned by the news.

~

"It's a boy!"

I was overwhelmed with love that defied logic. A warm, calming orb surrounded me as the nurse handed me my son. My baby boy was already my world. I looked up at Jason. He was wearing the flannel he'd worn the night of the car accident. It was becoming a badge of honor. He sobbed uncontrollably.

"It's a boy, a boy!" he yelled. "Gavin Luca, my son!" He wailed. But it wasn't touching, it was disturbing. The doctor looked at me, confused or concerned.

"His brother recently passed away. This is all just extra emotional for him," I explained. I couldn't help but notice people often looked at me that way—confused by my blindness, concerned for my well-being.

The day after we brought Gavin home, a couple of Jason's friends stopped by. They were all ushers in a friend's wedding that day. I was sleep-deprived, sore, and in a robe, but he wanted to show off the baby. "Men make men," he said. They laughed, drank beers, and headed out the door in tuxedos. "You good?" Jason asked as he looked back over his shoulder.

"My mother is on her way," I assured him, eager for him to leave.

That day marked the beginning of an endless parade of visitors. My Italian relatives stopped by day after day, night after night, to see the baby and offer congratulations. My mom came over to help with each visit like she was a hired waitress from a catering company. She mostly served coffee and pastries for our guests, sometimes lunch for certain ladies. The house needed to be spotless and well decorated; the visits were also to judge my home. It was what was expected in my family. I had to oblige.

In between the bustling visits, Jason's parents came over to spend time with the baby. Joanne had chopped off her hair and was frail as a wounded bird. She wasn't eating, and her head shook slightly as Jason handed her the baby. She stared down at Gavin cradled in her arms, my brother-in-law's absence the elephant in the room. Jason, his dad, and his stepdad kept forcing her to function as if nothing had happened, but she seemed disturbed by all the joy.

The different but equally strong energies of both families made me feel like I was living a split life. I exhausted myself trying to stay centered and find my strength as a new mother, as an adult woman, around all the chaos.

During one visit, Gavin was settled in his swing while Jason and I stepped outside with his dad to show him something new in our yard. Joanne sat across from the baby, in a trance on the living room couch. Once outside, we heard the door shut behind us. Bob and I immediately tried to open it, but we were locked out. We rang the bell and knocked on the door frantically, both worried about what Joanne might be capable of. We ran to the window to see what was going on. Gavin was out of his swing, but he and Joanne were not in sight. My heart raced.

"Kick down the door!" Jason's dad shouted at him. Before Jason responded, Joanne casually opened the door, holding the baby in her arms.

"What's all the commotion? I was just changing his diaper." She spoke through a sly grin. Jason kissed her forehead, as Bob and I exchanged a suspicious glance. I took the baby from her arms and retreated to the nursery, sat in the rocker, and held the baby close to my heart. I blamed myself for bringing him into a toxic environment. I felt the need to be with the baby at all times, as if my hypervigilant watch over him would protect him from any harm.

~

As maternity leave neared an end, I agonized over what to do with the baby when I went back to work. Jason and I didn't discuss it. I assumed I had to work and figure out childcare, while his job and routine stayed the same. I didn't want to put the baby in day care or hire a nanny. I feared it was unsafe. I had developed an irrational worst-case scenario anxiety disorder by then. My mom had summers off from her school office job. I knew I could rely on her when I first went back. I would cross each bridge as I got to it. Each time I overcame one obstacle, a new problem came to mind. Suddenly, the distance from my house to the city seemed like more than I wanted to take on. I had settled into suburbia without thinking through the commute to work with a young family.

"I was able to get a flexible schedule from my boss. I'm going to go to the city a few days a week and work from home the other days. Isn't that great?" I somehow sensed I had to sell this to Jason.

"Well, when you go to the city, I want my mother to watch the baby. I think it would be good for her," he countered.

I was agitated that he made it about his mother and paid no regard to me or the baby. "I don't think that's a good idea, given her condition. My mom said she could do it," I said.

"So you're going to try to keep my mother from the baby?" His tone turned hostile.

"Jason, your mother is on and off meds, and in and out of the psych hospital. She's had suicide attempts. I just don't feel comfortable." I couldn't believe he was asking this.

Jason scowled. "Her doctor told me that she's not suicidal. He doesn't even think she takes all the meds."

"I don't know what's worse, being suicidal or faking it." I didn't care what I said. No one was going to tell me what to do with my baby. "Either way, how can you think she's in any condition to babysit?"

"I'll tell you what I think. I think it's disgusting how insensitive and selfish you are," he sniped. "Have it your way for now . . . we'll see how it goes," he added.

chapter eight

WE DRESSED UP FOR ANOTHER SHOW ON THE MORNING OF Gavin's baptism. I had my hair and makeup done, and I wore a new outfit with heels. My anxiety had melted away the pregnancy weight. Jason wore a suit, gelled his hair, and finished his look with cufflinks. He went through the motions but did not seem to have the energy required to pull off the day. Gavin was dressed in a white suit imported from Italy that I'd picked out with my mom. He didn't appreciate the ridiculous hat on his head.

My brother-in-law would have been Gavin's godfather. Instead, my two childhood friends shared the role of godmothers. Joanne was dressed and propped up for pictures like a cardboard cutout. She clung to Bob, Jason's dad, as if she'd never divorced him, while her husband, Paulie, stood to the side, out of place. My parents radiated their typical combination of excitement and stress. Jason was not in the mood for the pomp of my family. His words were short, and he looked at me with a warning glare. The baptismal candle, typically held by the godfather during the church ceremony, repeatedly flickered out. This seemed to sour Jason's mood even more. My stomach was in knots from absorbing his tension.

We made our way with over one hundred friends and guests to the elegant restaurant we'd picked for the luncheon. The tables were set with blue floral centerpieces and place cards. Children were not invited to functions in my family. Jason's friends, un-aware of the *Moron Manual*, brought their babies. My mother was fearful that my relatives would be annoyed that only their children were excluded. I nervously apologized to a few cousins.

Paulie and Joanne were seated at the table next to us. Paulie had a few drinks in him. He lost his balance as he got up from the table and spilled a drink into our open diaper bag. Jason came back to the table and reached in the bag for his cigar case.

"Why's everything so wet?" he asked, annoyed.

"Paulie spilled his drink," I replied. I was trying to deflect his agitation off me, but my anxious maneuvering always backfired.

"He's such an asshole." Jason's anger was over the top.

"That asshole is taking care of your mother," Little Paulie snapped. He turned to his wife. "Let's go." He threw his napkin down on the table and walked through the restaurant toward the door.

Jason chased after him. "You have a problem? You want to settle it now, like a man?"

My cousin and my father moved between them. "Calm down!" my father yelled at Jason, trying to hold him back. Jason punched my dad in the face. My cousin and a few guests pulled my father and Jason off each other as Little Paulie exited out the door.

I stood in the middle of the restaurant, absorbing the scene. I'd grown accustomed to chaos by then. Friends looked shocked. Relatives seemed drawn to the drama. My mother sat with her head down, hand on her forehead, shoulders slumped. I tried to smooth the room over by discounting Jason's toxic behavior.

"He's having a very hard time," I whispered. "His brother

should have been the godfather today." I added, "His mom has been a lot for him to handle—just look at her." I believed sympathy from the guests would erase the guilt and shame I felt. Instead, I saw what by then had become a familiar stare of confusion and concern on most of their faces. Jason's friend took him outside to calm him down. My male cousins gathered around my dad to commiserate. No physical damage had been done; one of them had deflected Jason's arm and softened the blow. I tried to normalize the rest of the lunch by cutting the cake, taking pictures, and handing out blue chocolate crosses to the guests as they left, but the mood in the room was muted, subdued.

My parents waited for all the guests to leave and then left without saying goodbye to me. Jason and I drove home in silence. Once Gavin was sleeping in his crib, I hid in the basement and called my parents. I needed to undo the damage. I couldn't bear being such a disappointment.

"Hello?" My father sounded ready to commiserate with whoever would listen to his tale.

"Hello," my mother answered sternly at the same time from another receiver, as if she was expecting it to be me.

"It's me," I timidly said.

"What do you want, Francesca?" Her tone spoke volumes: *what's it going to take to fix you?*

"Is this son of a bitch hitting you?" my father asked before I could answer my mom.

"No," I shakily responded. He was shoving me around, pulling my hair, spitting on me, and bullying me. But he hadn't technically hit me.

"I always knew he was garbage," my father said, ignoring my response. "Paulie told me the day after the wedding that he thought Jason would abuse you. Paulie said he was a real piece of work." My father's tough-guy bravado annoyed me. I recalled watching my dad and Paulie walk around the yard at Joanne's brunch the day after our wedding. Something told me at the time that their conversation wasn't about golf. I wondered how many times I might have been saved from the misery of the past couple of years if someone had found the courage to speak up. I wasn't sure whether Paulie and my dad had been cowards or if they had chosen to mind their own business. Either way, they'd left me vulnerable.

"Benny, hang up!" my mother commanded with fierce anger. I heard the click of the receiver as my father hung up.

"Francesca, what kind of nonsense is this?" my mother started in. "I'm sick of this constant trouble with you and this loser. Bad enough we have to deal with him, now you humiliate me in front of the whole family? You better think long and hard about what you're doing over there, and straighten this mess out."

I wished she'd directed her anger at helping me start over. I needed to be parented again, healed, stabilized. Instead, she unintentionally pushed me to fix things with Jason. Leaving him now would add more shame to the scandal. It would mean leaving on a low, and I intuitively knew I had to leave on a high. I stood by my position that his outburst was out of character, a direct result of emotional stress following a horrific tragedy. We collectively brushed it under the rug, and life moved on. Jason never apologized, and no one mentioned the incident again. I shushed my desire to seek resolution and feel at peace. I understood the protocol was to fight and then let things blow over until anger boiled up again. I put a lid on my emotions and let them simmer, unexpressed.

~

On the last night of my maternity leave, my mind raced with woeful memories and projected dread on what was to come. I had spent a fitful night tossing and turning with anticipation and walked down to the nursery in the middle of the night. "Mommy has to go back to work tomorrow," I'd whispered to Gavin while he slept in his crib. I felt my first pang of mommy guilt and fear of separation. *Will he detach from me? Will he be safe?* I worried about getting myself and the baby ready. I worried about having the supplies packed. I worried about traffic. I worried about Gavin choking on his baby food.

I was already awake when my alarm clock buzzed at 6:00 a.m. I showered and dressed and loaded up the car with my work bag, diaper bag, and bouncy seat. I warmed a bottle for the ride. I gently lifted a sleeping Gavin from his crib and placed him on the changing table. His little body stretched as he yawned. He looked up at me and smiled drunkenly, still in a sleepy state. It broke my heart to think I was about to abandon him. Once his diaper was on and his onesie was snapped up, I buckled him in his car seat and began the one-hour drive in rush hour traffic to my parents' house. Jason stayed in bed.

Traffic was bumper-to-bumper. Halfway through the ride, Gavin began to fuss. My heart raced, and I began to sweat.

"What's the matter, little man?" I tried to soothe him. His fussing turned to crying. I kept one hand on the wheel while I opened his bottle and reached back to feed him. I had to keep my right arm extended to the back seat until he was done, because he wasn't holding a bottle on his own yet. I finally arrived at my parents' house. They were excitedly waiting on their porch. My dad unloaded the car while I went into the kitchen with my mom and Gavin. I rattled out a list of instructions on how to care for him. I showed her the supplies in the diaper bag as if she wouldn't see them unless I named each item. I handed Gavin to my mom, and he reached for her face and smiled. Their connection comforted but irritated me. I did not want to leave my son for a job that meant nothing to me, and I was annoyed with myself for having to depend on my parents as if I were a child again.

I walked a few blocks to my old bus stop and began the second leg of my commute to the office. I was wiped out from what already felt like a full day. I perked up when I ran into some old friends and neighbors; their warmth and familiarity energized me. But my mood turned melancholy as I stared out the bus window. I longed to be somewhere else, to be doing something else, to be free with Gavin. But I just couldn't seem to move from where I was. Nothing changed; it just got more complicated.

Back at the office, I greeted my coworkers in much the same way I had after the honeymoon and anniversary trips. I was genuine when I gushed about Gavin, but the rest of my life remained a secret farce. I called my mom incessantly and spent the day anxiously waiting for it to be over.

I commuted back to my parents' house and found my brothers, sister-in-law, and grandmother huddled around Gavin's high chair. My mother was at the stove while my dad read the newspaper. We'd slipped into our usual roles and banter. I joined right in but felt out of place at the same time. I didn't quite belong anywhere. I longed to recognize my place, to feel right. I drove home, again in over an hour of traffic, listening to a tape of baby music. Jason wasn't home to help me in; he'd left a message saying he was at his mother's.

I went through this routine for the next few months. I thought my work-from-home days would be a huge relief. In some ways they were—at least I didn't have to endure the long commute. But trying to juggle the baby and my job was a stressful circus act. I got up early to start my day before Gavin woke up. I frantically accomplished as much as possible before I heard him stir. I fed and played with Gavin while stressing about the work I had to get back to. I worked while feeling guilty for not being fully attentive to the baby. My mom came over often. She took Gavin for walks while I squeezed in more time at my computer, and she fed him while I took calls. She left before Jason came home. Her help made life bearable, enabling me to stick it out and carry on.

chapter nine

"THERE ARE WOMEN WHO WOULD GIVE THEIR RIGHT ARM TO BE you." The doctor handed me a tissue box so I could dab my tears and blow my nose.

"I know," I replied, ashamed. Gavin wasn't even four months old, and I'd just learned I was pregnant again. I felt guilty as I looked at him in his stroller, as if I were denying him attention by bringing another baby into the picture. I feared I wouldn't be able to love him like he deserved. I think I also feared I was digging myself deeper into life with Jason.

Jason was excited by the news. He and his brother were exactly a year apart. He didn't seem stressed about adding another baby to the mix. After all, I was doing all the work. He seemed to enjoy photo opportunities and bragging rights when it came to Gavin. The rest was up to me. The commute to drop off Gavin before heading to the city was more exhausting with the new pregnancy. I asked Jason if he could at least help me get out the door in the morning. "I have a quality-of-life job," he replied. "I don't need to be up that early." I guessed he was still punishing me for having my mom babysit instead of his. My insides burned with rage. My pent-up resentment fueled superhuman action. I was determined to find the strength to do it all, in spite of Jason. I refused to let him, or his mother, get the best of me. I refused to shortchange Gavin in any way.

The news of the second pregnancy seemed to increase Joanne's desire to cause friction between Jason and me. She manipulated him to tend to her and complained about me to him. She could do no wrong in his eyes, and we continued to have fights instigated by her.

Whenever Joanne came over to visit, Jason invited his dad over too. Jason and Joanne were fixated on pretending they were an intact family. Bob was happy to be included but did not appreciate the dynamics at play among Jason, Joanne, and me. The tension in the air was palpable. Bob did not make eye contact with Joanne. He looked at me with sympathy and shot Jason questioning looks. He would abruptly leave in the middle of a visit, his growing irritation obvious. I hated having Joanne at my house so much that I found myself relieved when Jason went to see her instead.

One night, Jason came home angry from a visit with Joanne. He brushed by me and grabbed the phone.

"Dad? Mom tells me you aren't taking her calls. With everything I'm dealing with, I have to listen to this bullshit?" He pursed his lips and flared his nostrils while he listened to Bob's reply.

He paced the kitchen floor. Regardless of what Bob was saying, Jason was prepared to respond. "You can't do me the favor of being there for her? You can't find it in you to comprehend what this woman is going through?" He nodded his head. "I'll tell you what. If you don't want to talk to her, you don't get to talk to me." He hung up.

This was not the first time I witnessed this dynamic. I'd seen Joanne complain to Jason about Bob over the years, pitting Jason against his dad until they wound up temporarily estranged. As manipulative as Jason could be, Joanne seemed to manipulate him. Or perhaps he enjoyed taking out his rage, and he used his mom's whining as an excuse to bully. The dynamic made my head spin. It was so obvious, yet Jason didn't seem to see it. Joanne seemed satisfied with her slick maneuvers and took no responsibility for her role in the dysfunction she created. I knew I could quickly be the next target. I already had been.

Bob called me one afternoon while I was working from home. He really wanted to see the baby. I felt for him. He'd lost one son to a tragedy indirectly caused by his ex-wife, and his older son cut him off to defend her. He was alone in his apartment, depressed. We made arrangements for him to visit midmornings on some days I worked from home. I could sneak him in while Jason was at his office, and he could spend time with Gavin. It worked for me too, because I could get some work done and give my mom a break once in a while.

During one visit, Bob sat in the rocking chair and rocked Gavin to sleep for his nap. I came into the nursery to check on them and found Bob overwhelmed with emotions.

"It's not easy," he said, referring to the son he'd lost. "There are days I wish I would die so I could see him again." He wept, then looked down at the baby. "But then I'm so thankful to see this little one."

"Anytime you want to stop by, just call me," I said. "I'll make sure we work around Jason."

"It's hard enough to hold it together when you're stable, but Joanne wasn't well before this all happened." He seemed to want to justify his decision to cut off his ex-wife. "I just can't be around her anymore; it's too much for me."

I didn't move. I sensed I was about to get an earful. "She's been screwed up since I met her. Her father beat her. He was an alcoholic, you know." I hadn't, but I nodded in acknowledgement. "Maybe that's why she's so messed up herself. I've tiptoed around her my whole life trying to avoid conflict so I could see my boys. I bit my tongue many times for fear of losing my sons." He choked back tears and added, "But now she killed one. I can't sit back and watch her destroy the other one's life. I see what's going on here. I see her destroying your marriage."

I took the sleeping baby from his arms and laid him in the crib. "Can I get you a coffee or anything?" I asked, feeling awkward. Bob's raw honesty was exactly what I longed for, but it felt peculiar to me. I'd been programmed to hide the truth and collude in dysfunction. He'd just pulled the curtain back, exposing Joanne's dark existence and my flawed marriage. I wasn't prepared to look.

"No, thank you. I'll be on my way. I really appreciate being able to visit like this." He wiped his face with a handkerchief.

After Bob left, I called my mom and told her what he'd said. We bonded over gossip and the validation we received from how messed up other people were. There was relief at first, followed by guilt. Deep down I knew it was a distraction from what bothered us about ourselves. After all, I must have been in a pretty screwed up emotional place myself if Jason and his mother were the people in my circle.

Emotions intensified as the holidays approached. There was a split energy between the baby's first Christmas and the first Christmas since my brother-in-law's death. Jason's anger intensified, and Joanne's nastiness seeped through her trance. The nastier she got, the more Jason stood by her side. I was enmeshed in the drama and pain.

One weekend, Joanne was over again, hanging out with Jason, ignoring me.

"Give me a few minutes to change, and then I'll be ready to go," he said to his mom.

"Now where are you going? I could use some help today," I complained as I held Gavin over my pregnant belly.

"Out with my mother," he informed me.

"Don't you think this is getting a bit much?" I prodded.

"Why don't you have one of your visitors come over to help you?" he replied, letting me know he was aware that my mom frequently came over during the week, and his estranged father too.

"Did you ever think I wouldn't need so much help if you weren't always running off to cater to your mother?" I snapped back.

"I'll tell you what I think." He came charging toward me while I was still holding Gavin. "I think you're nothing but a slut!" He spat in my face.

Before I could respond, Joanne called out from behind Jason, "You tell her, Jason Paul."

"You're sick!" I screamed at him.

I turned on Joanne. "And you're even sicker, because you raised him and encourage his abuse." I was overcome with a ferocious desire to expose them for the monsters they were.

They proudly walked out the door as if I were a lunatic who was beneath them. I was panting with rage when I realized Gavin was crying, looking at me with fear. His innocence and vulnerability struck a chord. Something in me shifted. Children learn what they live. I vowed to pull myself together and not darken his world. I soothed him and kissed him and told him a dozen times, "It's okay. Mommy's okay."

The baby was due early April 2001. I spent a late January day at my parents' while Jason was at a college basketball game with fraternity brothers. It was a help to have them play with Gavin, who was ten months and crawling around quickly. I felt a distinct labor pain as I got up from their couch. I ignored it, but it was soon followed by others. By the time Jason came to pick me up, I feared I was in labor. We went to the hospital and learned I was in fact having contractions and dilating in preparation for birth. The doctors were concerned. The baby was only twenty-nine weeks along. Jason seemed unfazed. He kept telling the nurse he hoped it was another boy.

"Men make men." He shared his offensive catchphrase with the nurse, who half-smiled, trying to be polite but not appreciating his humor and immaturity. They were able to give me some medication to stop the contractions and eventually send me home.

We went back to my parents' house to pick up Gavin. They looked very concerned when I explained what had happened.

"You need to stay off your feet," my mother said to me, but her words were directed at Jason.

"I'll make sure to take good care of her, Lily. Don't you worry," he said in a commanding tone.

I took a pill every four hours for the next several weeks to hold off labor. I was put on modified bed rest and worked from home. It was safe to stop the medication at thirty-six weeks. A few days later we were in the delivery room, welcoming our son Ben.

"Men make men!" Jason swaggered and crowed repeatedly. He was wearing the plaid shirt from the night of the accident again. He was such a jackass that I paid him no regard. I held Ben in my arms, and my heart expanded. I had another love of my life to protect. I couldn't wait for Gavin to meet his little brother. I needed the three of us close together as I slowly began to contemplate our escape.

chapter ten

VISIONS OF A TRANQUIL LIFE DANCED IN MY HEAD, BUT BETWEEN my job and the babies, now nineteen and seven months old, I was too busy managing everyday reality to create my daydreams. I was in the kitchen, heating up pastina on the stove, when Jason emerged from the bathroom in a tuxedo.

"Where are you going?" I asked, surprised to see him so dressed up.

"There's a party after the polls close," he replied. It was election night.

"I thought you were just going to club headquarters. Were guests invited?" I fell right into his trap.

"I assumed you knew. I'm taking my mother." He dismissed me. My body tensed. I didn't even want to go out with him; I wanted to be valued.

Jason had been campaigning for county legislator since the beginning of the summer. He was in no way projected to beat the beloved incumbent, but he did what was asked of him by his Republican Club and local politicians. He was their boy, or so they thought. In reality, he did favors for them so they would owe him. Joanne fed off it as if he were a prominent political icon. Night after night, they went door knocking while I was home with two babies, working from a basement office and taking care of the household. My hair was in a perpetual ponytail, my uniform a pair of denim shorts and a T-shirt stained with baby food.

I ran up and down the stairs all day, alternating between back-office basement accountant and mom of two. Gavin was just over a year, and Ben was only a few months old. I attended mommy-and-me classes in between monthly bank reconciliations, and pediatrician appointments in between performance reports. I cleaned the house, did the laundry, and grocery shopped with a double stroller. Jason dressed up in a suit but did the bare minimum at his job. He wore khaki pants and a Republican Club golf shirt as he walked the town with Joanne in the evenings. Afterward, they'd sit at my kitchen table for coffee.

"I have to make a call to headquarters," Jason mentioned through a yawn one evening.

"Jason Paul, how much can one person do?" Joanne moaned for him as I emerged from the basement to give the boys their baths. She grinned at me like I was the hired help.

I was fuming on the inside, but I would be damned if I gave them the satisfaction of knowing they'd irritated me. I made friends with other local moms and even spent a week in East Hampton with my family at my parents' rental house. I lounged around their built-in pool with the boys and strolled Main Street for dinner and ice cream in the evening. It was a slice of the charmed life Mom and I expected for me. I fit right into the fantasy world until the end of the week.

On election night, I snapped. That was the last time he and Joanne would make an ass out of me.

"You're taking your mother?" I roared.

"That's right. You have an issue with that?" He stood wide legged and stared at me.

"I'm your wife!" I reminded him.

"My mother supported my campaign," he shot back at me.

"Supported your campaign?" I couldn't believe what I was hearing. "What about me, working and taking care of the babies and the house while you were out parading around with her?"

"That's too bad for you." He smirked. "Now get out of my way so I can leave."

I was wild with rage. I grabbed a sneaker and threw it at him with all my might. He moved his face just in time, but it hit his neck. He pushed me into the refrigerator and held me up against it by the throat. I clawed at him and scratched his face. He shoved me to the floor and strode out the door.

I gathered myself to my feet, straightened my ponytail, threw out the burned pastina, and made mac and cheese for Gavin. The boys had been watching *Sesame Street* in the living room. Gavin was clenching a blanket and sucking on his binkie, staring wide-eyed at the TV. Ben was too young to notice anything from his bouncy seat. I gathered them at the kitchen table and fed them through mommy smiles while I seethed. My mind raced with plans for retaliation.

After I cleaned the kitchen, I called a locksmith to change the locks. Jason needed to learn his lesson. I needed him to grovel to prove my worth. Later that evening, I settled both boys to sleep after their baths and poured myself a glass of wine. Feeling empowered, I put my new keys in my bag and my feet up on the couch. I dozed off and woke to Jason trying to open the front door. I tiptoed toward it knowing I couldn't be seen and put my ear against it, expecting to hear him struggle. Instead, he chuckled and drove away.

Jason called me over the next couple of days, not for permission to come back home but simply to get his things. Frustrated that locking him out didn't seem to faze him, I refused to allow him in. His lack of remorse infuriated me. Determined to make my point, I dumped some of his stuff in the driveway, ran over the heap several times, and told him he could pick it up from there.

He showed up with a police escort. "Ma'am, your husband would like to remove his personal items from the marital home without incident," one of the two officers said when I opened the door. Jason stood behind them like he needed protection. Feeling mortified, I let them in. The officers and I stood in my kitchen in awkward silence while Jason gathered some things. I'd seen plenty of fights in my childhood home and had some wicked ones with Jason, but police in my kitchen took it to a whole new level. The sounds from their walkie-talkies, the flashing lights from their patrol car, and the holsters on their hips unnerved me.

"Thank you, officers," Jason respectfully said as he breezed by me with a duffel bag and a box.

"Ma'am." The policemen nodded at me as they followed him out. I stood there feeling like a crazy shrew while he strutted out the door.

My heart raced as I circled the kitchen, talking to myself in an effort to calm things down. I'd managed to survive up until then, surrounded by a sea of madness, but I was losing stamina. Frighteningly, it was the chaos that swelled within me that threatened to wash me away.

~

I gave Jason permission to visit the boys in our home for the next couple of months. It was a bridge between my fear of divorce and my desire to be free. Hell-bent to claim my power and control, I naively thought this meant he was at the mercy of my rules. I assumed he'd change his behavior and beg for forgiveness, and I would prove I was capable of fixing my life. I believed my ability to persevere through pain was a strength. It was really a way to hold things together for fear of how bad they could get.

We played the in-and-out husband/dad game for a while. He'd show up in a suit after work, eat dinner with us, entertain himself with the boys for a bit while I cleaned up, and then head back out the door. I had the house and the kids; he had the freedom to come and go like a college boy. We took out our hate for each other by indulging in the power these roles provided.

I thought I set myself free when I changed the locks. Moments of quiet in my living room alone late at night made me believe I was at peace. But my life was still full of chaos and drama, playing out in new ways. Some nights, Jason flirted with me, and my skin crawled with shame as if I were a whore. Other nights, we fought over bills that were due and who would be responsible for paying them. His unruffled, self-possessed nature intimidated me. He commanded power in his suits as I weakened in house clothes. He stirred fear in me. I fretted over my every move. I didn't know where he stayed at night. I didn't know what his intentions were. I didn't know what my fate would be. We didn't discuss our separation or plans to divorce. I anxiously waited for the next problem to show up for me to manage.

Ben required lots of medical attention during his first year. His head tilted to one side because of stiff muscles, and he needed physical therapy to help him move his neck. He also suffered from chronic ear infections and eventually needed ear tubes. I made sure to tell Jason about the endless appointments. I walked a tightrope between freeing myself of him and keeping him involved enough not to incite his wrath. I desperately hoped to spark empathy in him so he wouldn't torment me. Jason showed up for appointments like a concerned dad, always in a suit. He'd take a seat near us in the waiting room and lean forward in his chair with his legs spread wide apart as if ready to attack. He exaggerated his interactions with the boys to emphasize that he was ignoring me. He'd take cell phone calls and step away to whisper with a big smile on his face.

He turned on the charm in the exam rooms. "Yes, Doctor. Thank you, Doctor," he'd say with humble respect. "Understood. We'll make sure that's what we do," he'd say with feigned sincerity, even though he wasn't doing a darn thing.

"You hear that, little buddy—you're going to be okay," he'd say as he brushed Ben's cheek.

On the way out, we'd stop at the reception desk to settle up copays. Jason lurked behind me but never paid a bill. A particular pediatric otolaryngologist appointment totaled $650 out of pocket. I looked at him, and he patted his pants to indicate he didn't have his wallet. I cut a check from my purse. Ben's ear tubes cost close to $2,000. Jason didn't reimburse me a dime.

I was constantly twisted in knots from frustration. I couldn't figure out how to manage Jason in order to better my outcome. I tried to keep him close enough to soften him yet far enough to be free of him. But no matter what I did, he played me for a fool. He seemed to enjoy watching me spin like a top he played with until I spun out of control or broke. I shouldn't have provided so much entertainment; he would have gotten bored with me.

I had lost any ability to live in the moment and enjoy life by then. I apprehensively anticipated the next time there'd be a chance of conflict with Jason. I tiptoed around like a frightened mouse, not sure which way to move to avoid the pouncing cat.

The anxiety seeped into all facets of life. I feared accidents and tragedies. I believed the world was a dangerous place, and I ran on high alert, especially when it came to protecting my boys.

~

As the holidays approached, I agonized over how to handle Christmas being separated. I sold Jason on the suggestion of Christmas morning together as a family, trying to keep some sort of dynamic I could manage. I figured if I tossed him a bone in the morning, I'd be free to spend the rest of the day with the boys and my family. He went along with my enthusiastic plan so easily that his lack of resistance concerned me.

The doorbell rang on Christmas morning.

"Merry Christmas," I forced myself to say to Jason even though I despised him.

Jason brushed my shoulder as he stormed by me into the living room. The boys were on the floor surrounded by gifts from Santa. Jason was empty-handed. He hadn't offered to chip in for gifts or helped me shop during the weeks leading up to Christmas. I was annoyed that I had gone out of my way to buy him gifts from the boys. He took over the tiny living room, hovered over the boys, and positioned himself to block me out. He took pictures and smiled with a faraway look about him, as if the current arrangement was only temporary. He eventually gathered his gifts without any display of shame or gratitude, kissed the boys goodbye, and left without acknowledging me. I resented having him over and tried to chalk his cameo up as a waste of my time. But a dreadful worry hovered over me. A lingering energy in the air told me Jason was patiently waiting for a plan to unfold.

~

He conspicuously disappeared for a few days before calling me to start up his in-home playdates again. He dropped a duffel bag at the door as he barged into the kitchen, claiming his territory after coming back from a trip. The bag was strategically unzipped to expose a box of opened condoms. I took a step back, stunned to learn I wasn't the one dominating our separation. I was a fool doing all the work while he got to go out and enjoy single life. I took short labored breaths to control myself. I needed a way to establish my authority without giving him the satisfaction of knowing I had seen the condoms, but I was too reactive to hide my hand. I aggressively slammed cabinets and closed drawers as I tended to the stove. Jason walked around with a big smile, mocking me. My rage intensified

"The cell phone and mortgage bills are due," I snapped at him.

He played peekaboo with Ben, who was in his high chair, and ignored me.

"Put Gavin in his booster seat," I ordered. "Dinner's ready."

He grabbed a beer from the fridge and stepped out of the kitchen to make a call. I helped Gavin sit in his chair myself and began to feed the boys. He made his way to the table and stuffed his face with the dinner I had paid for and made.

My blood boiled. "Give the boys their bath while I clean up," I demanded.

"Can't tonight. Gotta run." He wiped his mouth and left the napkin on the table. He planted exaggerated kisses on the boys' foreheads. I was shaking with fury, and I dropped the pasta bowl. Sauce splattered everywhere.

"Good luck with that," he said, chuckling as he walked out the door.

~

I stewed for days. Jason showed up at the door for his nightly visits, but I refused to let him in. He rang the bell and knocked a few times as if making a valiant effort before he casually drove away. Moments later, like clockwork, the phone would ring. I refused to answer, but his countless messages pervaded. "Fran, I'm trying to see my sons. I know we have our differences, but I need to see the boys," he'd recite in a patronizing tone.

After about two weeks, a lanky guy with long matted hair and a dirty shirt knocked on my door.

"Can I help you?" I asked through the window, sensing trouble.

"You Francesca Axcel?" he asked.

"Yeah."

"I got this for you." He held up a manila envelope with my name in black Sharpie and a court stamp on the top left corner.

I cracked open the door, and he thrust the envelope toward me. I tore it open with trembling hands. Jason was suing me for divorce three months after I changed the locks. It was wishful thinking on my part to believe I could live between a blurred line of marriage and freedom. He claimed I had physically and emotionally abused him over the years. He'd filed a police report on election night to prove I was physically violent, as evidenced by the bruise on his neck and scratch on his face. He further cited that he'd needed a police escort to safely get his belongings from the home after I changed the locks. He referenced his brother's death as a play on sympathy, portraying me as an insensitive monster during a time of tremendous grief for him and his family. He was seeking a divorce and custody of the boys based on my refusal to allow him any time with them.

I felt stunned as I read the petition. After everything that had happened, *I* was the defendant? He'd spun a very twisted version of reality. It was a fabricated tale, yet he swore to it as truth and documented it formally in a court petition, which made it seem true. I panicked. I felt a desperate, urgent need to tell my side of the story. I wanted to scream and plead, "Doesn't anyone see what he's doing? Can't anyone help me get away from him? Can't anyone save me from his manipulation?" I needed people to understand I was the victim. I needed to be set free. I read the petition again, and the enormity of the accusations set in. I felt the heaviness of failure. My insides tightened as I realized my life was about to get even messier.

chapter eleven

IT TURNED OUT I WAS HANDED A LIFELINE WHEN I WAS SERVED
with divorce papers. I came alive, relishing my freedom and em-
bracing being single the way I should have in my twenties. I
joined a gym, started to get my hair blown out, and wore cute
clothes. It was so easy to look and feel good at thirty-one.

The divorce proceedings got underway, and Jason exercised
visitation on certain weeknights for dinner and Sundays for the
day. The boys were too young for overnight visits, and Jason
didn't have a place of his own. He'd been alternating between his
mother's couch and a friend's couch. I used the little free time I
had to keep myself and the home in order.

Some Sundays, when the weather was nice, I'd enjoy brunch
or outdoor drinks and live music with friends. "Where are you
girls from?" a guy asked us one afternoon at a bar on Prospect Isle.

"Queens," we said in unison.

"I work with a couple of guys from Queens," he replied. "You
guys know Joe Mulligan and Chuck Maloney?"

I nearly died. Chuck Maloney was *my* Chuck. The guy worked
as a police officer at Chuck's precinct.

"Oh, we know them," Michele said as she and Nicole giggled.
"Francesca knows Chuck well."

"Wait, you're *Francesca*?" he asked. I smiled and nodded.
"Chuck talked about you until the day he got married," he added.

My heart warmed, thankful for the random brush with my young love. I'd been grieving for months since I learned he got married. I'd even looked up his wedding registry to judge his wife's taste. It seemed unfair that I wound up available after he committed to her. I sipped my drink as I pined over the road not taken.

Mom and I were eager for me to have another chance at life. She babysat so I could go out with friends or dates on the weekends. I enthusiastically trekked into New York City to great restaurants, bars, and rooftop drinks. The city electrified me. The anonymity and endless possibilities lifted my spirits. Suburbia melted away for the night, and the world turned clear as if I'd just put on glasses for the first time. I had guiltless sex with a friend from college and felt like my own woman for the first time in my life.

The surge of energy and happiness spilled into my mommy world. The boys and I enjoyed playdates with neighbors and friends and pool parties and days at the beach. Gavin and Ben were silly and full of laughter. Life with them meant games and ice cream, giggles and wonder. We had so much fun; their childhood seemed playful and carefree despite the divorce.

I also got together with my friend Contessa and her baby daughter a lot. Our friendship had been rooted in college fun and shared backgrounds, and it blossomed into a lifelong bond colored with motherhood, womanhood, humor, and dreams.

I was single and free while wrapped up in the joy of parenting. But Jason wouldn't leave me alone. Instead of a mutually agreed upon no-contest divorce, there were countless court appearances and lawyer meetings dragged out over more than two years. He made it challenging, if not downright impossible, for us to amicably settle differences that came up around parenting our children. We were barely on speaking terms, and I lived in a state of constant hypervigilance, wondering what he was going to do next.

Jason's persistent attempts to turn routine matters into a made-for-TV court drama disoriented me. During a blackout in August 2003, Gavin ran a very high fever. We had no power, and I spent the night cooling him with ice water in the tub by flashlight. Ben was clammy and warm the next morning. I called Jason to explain they couldn't go out for dinner because they were ill. He showed up that night with a police escort and filed a petition that he'd been denied visitation with the boys.

Another time, the boys and I went to Disney World with my parents for a few days. I told Jason where we were staying, and he spoke to the kids every day while we were away. I came home to a court petition and a police report claiming Jason did not know the whereabouts of our children.

His nonsense annoyed me to no end, as did the fact that the police and courts indulged it. We had more appearances before the bench than some attorneys, thanks to Jason's endless legal motions. My imagination ran wild with worry about my every move and how he might twist it. My eyes darted back and forth in search of Jason's Jeep or cop cars wherever I went. He parked outside and waved at me when I went out with friends, and he showed up in parking lots when he'd spoken to the boys and learned where we were headed.

"We got a new fish, Daddy. We're going to Petco to get the fish food now," they told him over the phone.

We bumped into him while we shopped at Petco.

"We're going to Rosa's for pizza tonight, Daddy," they shared on another call.

He showed up to order a pie at the counter while we ate in our booth.

He waited in the nursery school parking lot each morning and followed me into the building to drop the boys off.

"Does it bother you that I'm here?" he once whispered in my ear as I helped the boys out of their car seats. I wished he would move on. His presence made me the subject of gossip among the other mothers. He played on my shame and fear of judgment, without regard for his impact on the boys.

Jason's tormenting and the contentious divorce proceedings took a toll on me. I started to think about moving to the city or at least back to Queens to get away from him. It made no sense for me to stay on Prospect Isle. My mom had to drive out to babysit, and I had to travel in the opposite direction to get into the city for office meetings or socializing. I was getting sick of working primarily out of my basement, limiting my professional and personal opportunities. Management had recently announced the firm was being sold, which prompted me to look for a new job in the city. On top of that, the stigma of being a single mom in suburbia annoyed me. I was lost between traditional families who didn't know where to place me and single men who couldn't see past minivans and playgrounds.

The writing was on the wall, but Mom didn't want me to sell the house. The disgrace of my failed marriage was a lot for her to bear. She dreaded judgment more than she dreaded Jason. The blemish on me was a blemish on her. She feared people would snicker that I couldn't afford to keep the house, and judge me for cramming into a city rental with the boys. She convinced me the boys needed to stay in their home. "It's a sin," she would say when I brought up the idea of moving. I was so tied to the *Moron*

Manual myself that I stayed put, afraid to venture outside my comfort zone. The devil I knew wound up being far worse than the devil I feared.

chapter twelve

ALMOST TWO YEARS AND $75,000 INTO THE DIVORCE PROCEEDINGS, I sat at my kitchen table with my head in my hands, staring at the latest legal bill. I couldn't afford to pay it, but I had to or my attorney wouldn't give my case much attention. He hadn't returned my latest call and did not share my urgency or desperation regarding Jason's antics. My case was my universe, but to him I was just another client with the same old story and an outstanding invoice.

My mind raced, trying to figure out how to come up with the money. I had to work, but I refused to be away from the boys all day, making money at a job I didn't like only to pay unwanted expenses such as legal fees. My income was limited to what I could earn working flex hours from home. In theory, I had the ideal setup for a working mom with two small children. In reality, I walked a tightrope between full-time parenting and flex-time accountant, and lived with constant guilt of never being good enough at either.

I spent a lot of mental energy planning and organizing my life, as if it were a challenge I had to overcome. I wrote lists for my lists, rewriting them when I crossed off a task. I filled in the calendar with scheduled activities and plans, to convince myself I was in control of things. I had a laundry day, a grocery shopping day, and a five-year plan. I thought I was keeping ahead of things and protecting myself from unwanted circumstances, but in reality I was reacting poorly to the latest mess created by my fear-based decisions. I convinced myself I was a victim of an unkind world, doubting my circumstances had anything to do with my choices. Instead of changing careers, cutting expenses, or seeking some other way to support myself and the boys, I folded my arms and pouted at the injustice of it all.

The quick fix: ask my father. He had already cut multiple checks to fund my divorce proceedings with Jason. I withered thinking about it, but I had already wiped out my 401k and maxed out several credit cards. I could sell the house and move to a more affordable apartment, but my mother had me convinced that was a step backward. Despite all the emotional drama growing up, I never wanted for anything. Material pleasures compensated for my insecurities. I feared if I sold the house for something more affordable, it would confirm I was inadequate. I had already gone through so much money from my father, I figured a little more wouldn't make a difference. The thought of asking him made me squirm. I knew from prior experience that he would give me the money and then humiliate me for needing it.

"The divorce is costing me more than the wedding," he joked with his friends in front of me and, I'm sure, behind my back.

"NYU tuition was cheaper than this," he'd quip, a not-so-subtle reminder that he'd paid my tuition, even though he told me at the time not to worry about the cost.

He wasn't as good-humored behind closed doors. He complained to my brothers about giving me money to pay lawyers, painting a picture that I was bleeding him dry. They resented me for taking the money, and I was furious at their self-righteousness. Dad made similar complaints about them. He frequently ranted to me that he bailed Luca out of gambling debt, and paid for Dominick's extravagant wedding and set him up with a lucrative career. He bonded with one of us kids by bashing the others. My brothers and I went through periods of time in which we didn't speak to one another because of the animosity between us.

My parents bonded in the war against Jason, a distraction from their own misery. My divorce wasn't just about the issues between me and Jason; it was generations of pain from both families playing out through us. Determined to win the fight, Dad eagerly handed me checks to cover the costs, knowing that I wouldn't be able to pay him back. He didn't want me to; he wanted to be a big shot. I hated myself for taking it, and I hated him for giving it to me, but I feared what life would be like if I didn't. The more he gave me, the more I relied on him and resented the hold I thought he had on me. He unapologetically opened my mail and snooped through my drawers, rationalizing that he'd bought the right to know my personal business. I refused to acknowledge that I had put myself in that position. I longed for freedom and blamed everyone else, especially my parents and my ex-husband, for my lack of it.

For years, I exploded in fits of rage that often shocked me. My worst outburst was triggered during a phone call with my father, ten years after my divorce and a few months after my mom's death. He was trying to weasel his way out of recent bad behavior.

"You know the costs of Mom's care were through the roof. I'm thinking maybe you and your brothers could contribute toward it," my father said.

"Are you serious?" I couldn't believe he was playing the poor guy card. His request felt punitive. "You had insurance to cover everything." I said, not willing to let him play me.

"I guess you forgot about all the money I had to give you for court." He tried to lay on the guilt.

"Oh, now you're going to make it about that?" I challenged.

"That's right, I am. You just take and take and never show me any respect."

My jaw clenched, and my grip on the phone receiver tightened as I tried to hold back my rage. My mind filled with memories of his manipulation, lies, and blame to cover his own guilt. I trembled uncontrollably,

"I'm sick of listening to you throw money in my face!" I finally screamed, unable to stop myself. I hated him, and he hated me for that.

I exploded. "I wouldn't have been in that marriage in the first place if I'd seen a normal relationship growing up! All the money you paid the lawyers was you paying your dues for the abuse you put us all through!" I was so worked up, I was out of my body, watching myself go berserk from a distance.

I added, "You're so sick, and you were so mean and abusive to us and Mommy!" I yelled so loudly I feared I would pop a blood vessel. I was trying so hard to finish my mother's fight and unload years of my own hate, I was barely coherent. "You made my mother sick, and you killed her, and I hate you for being the one that's still alive!" I said, seething.

"I can't stand you either, Francesca. If it wasn't for your kids, I wouldn't have anything to do with you." His words were full of venom.

"Good," I bellowed. "Do me a favor, and stay the hell out of my life!" I hung up.

Letting all that out felt good for a while, but the relief was short-lived. I feared I would never be rid of my anger. I wondered if my father would ever atone for his wrongdoings, thinking that would justify my rage and help me find some peace in my life. It took me a long time, a lot of pain, and a cancer diagnosis to realize that peace could only come from within myself.

Although I wasn't yet in that mindset at my kitchen table all those years ago, I had an inkling that inner peace and integrity were worth more than the money my father could give me. I'd have to find another way to pay the lawyer.

I looked in the Yellow Pages for a local jeweler, grabbed my wedding ring, and drove the short distance to a neighboring town. The store was right down the street from Jason's office. Even my most random choices, such as picking a jeweler from the phone book, seemed to conjure drama.

A bell chimed as I entered the store. A middle-aged man looked up from behind one of the glass cases.

"Hi. I'm interested in selling a diamond ring." I tried not to sound desperate.

He nodded. "I can take a look."

I pulled a small red box out of my bag and opened it on the counter. I waited for him to gasp as if I had presented him with the crown jewels, the rarest find. Instead, he seemed unimpressed.

"It's a little over three carats," I prompted, trying to convince him of its worth.

"That's not what matters," he said. He held it up to the light, twirling it in his fingers as my enthusiasm dimmed. "It's very flawed."

"That can't be," I countered, offended, even though I'd suspected this all along.

"Look how cloudy it is." He compared it to a clear diamond in his case. "See how dull the color is?"

My cheeks burned. There was no denying it: the ring was as flawed as the marriage.

"How much is it worth?" I asked.

"Six thousand dollars," he said as if he were doing me a favor.

"I'll take it," I replied. It wouldn't cover even half of the lawyer's bill.

I put the envelope of cash in my bag. As I walked toward my car, I felt revitalized, like I'd pawned off Jason and any evidence of my past mistakes. But my exhilaration was short-lived. The next morning, I called my dad and asked him for a check to cover my shortfall.

chapter thirteen

JASON'S LOVE FOR LITIGATION AND HIS STALKING BEHAVIOR were weighing on me. I eventually retained a new attorney, hoping she would quickly finish our divorce so I could get Jason out of my life, as if then all my problems would magically go away. Thankfully, the judge presiding over our case ultimately saw right through Jason's bogus claims. He awarded me full physical and legal custody of the boys. Jason would be able to exercise visitation rights, including overnights every other weekend.

Giving one parent full rights was practically unheard of at the time. Jason was left with no say in any decisions regarding the boys, who were now four and three. The judge knew Jason would interfere every step of the way. I agreed to buy Jason out of the house with a sizable amount of money from my dad in order to wrap up the process.

We had one more court appearance scheduled to finalize the divorce.

"Okay, quickly, before we're called," my attorney said as she sat next to me with a legal pad in her hands. "Full custody for you, and visitation for him. He'll pay child support based on his salary, which isn't much, but you're used to being the breadwinner anyway. You agreed to buy him out of the house and take full ownership." She looked at me to confirm.

"Sounds right," I said.

"Did you know his mother bought him a house three blocks from you?" she asked. "He's moving in there after this settles so he can start having his overnight visits."

"What?" I said, dismayed at the close proximity. "I had no idea. Wow, he needs to move on," I quipped.

"You sure you still want to buy him out and stay? Maybe you want to think about selling the house and putting a little distance between you. You have up to a fifty-mile radius," she advised.

I didn't want to go through the effort and expense of coming up with a new plan at the finish line. I signed the divorce papers, chalking Jason and Joanne up to two wackos who wouldn't be relevant in my life now that the divorce was final.

~

The court-appointed law guardian inspected Jason's tiny, trailer-like ranch home and made sure he had toddler beds and gates installed. It was part of the settlement terms to alleviate my concerns for their safety. The boys were eased into weekend sleepovers starting with one night for a while, until it gradually turned into every other weekend from Friday evening to Sunday evening. But Ben never got comfortable with the arrangement. Jason had Gavin on a pedestal. He played up Gavin's love of sports and his boyish personality while he picked on Ben, who was more artistic. I started to see signs of deep hurt in Ben and a wedge forming between the boys. My blood boiled as this silent poison seeped into their childhood. I resented the visitation agreement. Mommy guilt and fear plagued me. I worried about the boys and felt like I was betraying them every time they went to stay with Jason. I always sent them to his house with bags packed with fresh clothes, cozy pjs, Gavin's puppet Herbie, and Ben's blankie. Jason returned the bag with dirty laundry. Usually some items were missing.

Shortly after Jason began weekend visits with the boys, his girlfriend moved in. She was divorced with a boy and two girls herself. She had bleached blonde hair with hot pink highlights, and tattoos visible beneath scanty outfits. Her kids seemed to stay mostly at their dad's at first. But Jason began grooming them into a perfect little family. He tried to clean up her image by getting her an office job at the town municipal offices where he worked, where nepotism ran deep. Her kids eventually moved in with them and transferred to the top-ranked school district where we lived. Jason portrayed himself as father of the year by coaching every activity and showing up at every school event with his mother and new family in tow. People fell for his Daddy of the Year act, but I knew it was contrived. He seemed to be laying the groundwork to get back at me for having full custody and was willing to use the boys to do so. My anxiety intensified, and I realized my happy single life had been built on sand.

The more off-center I felt, the more off-center things got. The college friend I'd been having a fling with got engaged to his old girlfriend mere days after we had a fun evening and great sex. His interest in me stopped at my suburban mom fence. We weren't even dating, so the devastation I felt revealed how broken I was. I feared I would never find love or stability or peace. I realized I wouldn't be able to wipe my marriage to Jason from my slate. A divorced dad could move on, but a divorced woman had baggage. I cried in my bed late that night and called Chuck at work. The officer who answered the phone said he wasn't on duty at the time. Chuck never returned my call. I felt ashamed and humiliated, pathetic.

~

Memorial Day weekend approached, and I resented not having an intact family, including a devoted husband, to share it with. My married friends had family plans, and my single friends headed to beach homes in party towns. I refused to be stuck blowing bubbles around an inflatable pool in my backyard while eating mac and cheese. I felt the boys and I deserved a fuller life. I complained to my mother about how unfairly things had turned out for me. She had my dad book us all a trip to a luxury resort on Marco Island. I was ashamed, but I justified the lavish perks from my parents as restitution for their dysfunction. I blamed them for the mess I was in. It was the least they could do.

I came home tanned and ready to start a new job in New York City I'd been offered right before the trip. My resume painted me as an ambitious professional, even though I had no interest in my field. I was so used to pretending to be someone I wasn't, the interview process was a piece of cake. I negotiated a flexible work schedule at a firm in desperate need of staff. This meant I needed a sitter early in the morning a couple of days a week so I could make the train. My mom worked in a school, so early mornings didn't work for her. Jason had calmed down a bit by then; he seemed magnanimous in my diminished spirits. I mistook the calm for a truce. I asked him to watch the boys the mornings I had to catch the train. Deep down, I hoped the amicable gesture would keep me safe from his wrath. I think he relished my naivete. He'd come over just in time for me to run out the door so we didn't have to interact much. I made sure to lock my bedroom and office so he couldn't rummage through my things. Jason gave the boys breakfast, put Gavin on the bus, and drove Ben to nursery school before he had to be at his job. My mom picked the boys up after school and watched them until I came home.

The first day at my new job, I felt exhilarated walking the city streets on my way to the office. I was committed to achieving the perfect superhuman blend of devoted mom and single professional. I planned to meet college friends after work, so I had dressed up a little bit more than usual. My boss took me around the office to introduce me to my colleagues. He knocked on an open office door, and the man behind the desk looked up. For a moment he looked irritated by the interruption, but his expression quickly changed to interest.

Richard introduced me. "Theo, this is Francesca Miracola. She joined us today in the Hedge Group."

Theo got up from behind his desk to shake my hand. He was tall and slender but muscular. His hair was a bit too long for financial services, but I appreciated the unconventional nuance.

"Nice to meet you," he said. His big hazel eyes widened as his brows raised, indicating he was excited to have me onboard.

"Likewise," I replied, acknowledging the immediate attraction between us.

We flirted a bit at a firm happy hour a few weeks later, and soon afterward he asked me to lunch. The chemistry between us was intense, and we started dating almost immediately. I felt attractive, independent, energized, and fun when I was with him.

Jason soon suspected I was dating. The boys must have told him that I sometimes came home late. He began to leave flirtatious notes on the kitchen counter about how good I looked on my way to work.

One day, Jason had to pick the boys up from school and stay with them until I got home from work because my mom couldn't make it. I came home that night to find Jason had rummaged through the laundry basket in the bathroom and hung my lace underwear throughout the house. I felt violated and repulsed. I called him immediately and told him I no longer needed him to babysit. I hired a local mom to get the boys to school. Jason was furious that I was "denying him access" to his mornings with the boys. He had his regular visitation schedule; the extra mornings were a gift. I refused to give in.

My mom continued to watch the boys after school. Some days she took them to tennis lessons, the one activity Jason didn't coach. He showed up in his suit and sat on the bench and cheered. He chatted with the coach and helped the boys gather the balls from the court. He smirked and walked with them out to my mom's car. She seethed over this more than I did.

"That fat bastard was at tennis again today," she'd rant as soon as I walked through the door. Jason's boxy build had grown wider, rounder, and softer. His puffy head seemed to rest on his white collar as if he had no neck at all.

"Just ignore him," I'd reply like I was beyond it all.

"It's not right, Francesca. You work all day and pay for the lessons, and you're not there but he is?" Jason was supposed to cover 50 percent of all extracurricular expenses, but he rarely did. It was like trying to get blood from a stone.

"What would you like me to do?" I asked, frustrated. Instead of doing what made sense regarding where to live or work or how to create a peaceful life with my boys, I stayed stuck in dysfunction. My mom left my house aggravated. She was stuck and unable to free me, the same way she'd been unable to free herself. We sprinkled glitter over reality whenever we could and spoiled the kids to overcompensate for our guilt. The more we tried to get through with smiles on our faces and toys for the kids, the more Jason inserted himself, making us scramble like mice in a maze.

My dad and his friend spent hours putting together a basketball hoop my parents bought for my driveway. Gavin was thrilled, and even Ben had fun taking some shots. Jason began shooting hoops every time he came to pick up the boys. I'd stand with my arms folded at my kitchen door, full of rage. I was furious at such nonsense as a basketball hoop, enraged that I couldn't seem to establish boundaries.

The more I let Jason bother me, the further he pushed. He began showing up at the school frequently, sometimes even waving in the boys' classroom windows, until the school administrators informed him that he could only be on school property for official school business. At least I knew I wasn't crazy, but I still didn't know how to break free of him. He showed up unannounced at the house constantly, pretending the boys had forgotten something. He was making his presence known in much the same way a dog pees on his territory.

～

One night, I was grilling at my barbeque when Jason startled me at the gate. He'd dropped the boys off the night before from his visitation, after I'd just spent the weekend away with Theo.

"Ben forgot this." He held up Ben's blankie. "Can I come in and say hello to the boys?" he asked.

"It's not a good night. I have company over," I lied instead of just saying no, hoping it would make him go away. The boys hadn't met Theo yet, but I figured if Jason thought a man was in the house, he wouldn't bully me so much.

"You're a nasty bitch!" He dropped all pretense of niceties as soon as he realized he wasn't going to get what he wanted.

Once when the boys and I were in the Hamptons with my parents, we ran into childhood neighbors from Queens. One of them was also Jason's fraternity brother.

"These are your sons?" he asked.

I introduced them. "Yes, this is Gavin, and this is Ben."

He laughed and noted how much they resembled my brothers. "I heard you and Jason split up."

"You heard right."

"I never understood why you married him in the first place. I had fun with my fraternity, but man, he was the one guy so many of us despised."

I smiled as if to thank him for siding with me, but inside I hummed with anger at yet another person who hadn't spoken up. But I quickly realized there wasn't much he could have done. We were just casual acquaintances.

The next day, I was driving with my parents, wedged in the back between two booster seats, listening to them bicker in the front seat. We were stuck in traffic and running a little behind for Jason's dinner with the boys. I called him from my cell and said we'd be late. We arrived at my house to find Jason waiting outside with police officers. He claimed he had no idea where we were and that he hadn't seen or heard from his boys in days.

I'd had it with everyone by then—Jason, my parents, police officers, people who knew I shouldn't have married Jason. I rolled my eyes and blamed them all for being nuts, refusing to acknowledge that I participated in the madness. I escaped it by living a double life with Theo, dating him in a vacuum from the rest of my world. I liked who I was without having to deal with outside influences. I ran off to the city every other weekend, free to act as I pleased.

~

After we'd been dating for over a year, I invited Theo to spend a weekend with the boys and me in Montauk. Our relationship was growing more serious, but I hadn't introduced the boys to him yet. I wasn't sure how a bachelor with no children would fare with a six- and five-year-old, but I was ready to find out.

"He's taller than the refrigerator," Gavin said as Theo carried our bags to the car. He and Ben were excited to meet Mommy's friend.

We arrived at our rental unit, and Theo stayed behind to watch a horse race while I ran out to get lunch with the boys.

"Why didn't your boyfriend come to lunch with us?" Ben asked.

"He's not her boyfriend, Ben. He's her friend," Gavin said.

"Oh, she likes him," Ben added. At five years old, he was astute.

We had a great weekend. Theo and the boys enjoyed one another, and my relationship with Theo grew more serious. He started spending time with us as a family, and I contemplated the possibility of a future with him.

And then Jason went full throttle.

chapter fourteen

GAVIN RAN FROM JASON'S CAR TOWARD MY FRONT DOOR, SOBBING, after a weekend visitation.

"What's the matter?" I asked.

"We can't find Herbie," he said, crying. Herbie the hand puppet was Gavin's right-hand man.

I looked up toward Jason, who was standing at the curb. He dismissed me with a disdainful look. "He'll turn up, buddy—don't you worry," he yelled toward Gavin as he got into his car and drove away.

Gavin was inconsolable. He cried himself to sleep and went to school depressed the next day. My heart hurt for him. I called Jason to ask if he'd found the puppet but got no response.

Gavin sulked over dinner and barely ate. I did my best to comfort him to sleep, but he had another hysterical night. The next day, I searched the Internet for another Herbie, ordered one, and came up with a plan.

When Jason came to pick up the boys for dinner, I walked to the curb and spoke to him through the car window. "Did you find Herbie?" I asked.

"No, no I didn't." He exaggerated disappointment.

"I ordered a new one that will get shipped any day. I'm going to give it to Gavin and tell him a family found him, cleaned him up, and located his home." Jason stared straight out the front window with his hands on the steering wheel. "So if you find the original soon, let me know. Otherwise I'll tell you when I give him the new one, so if you ever find the old one, don't give it to him." He just continued to stare.

"Okay?" I asked. "Jason?"

"I heard you. Where are the boys?"

I walked back into the house to get them, and they left for dinner.

Eventually new Herbie arrived. Gavin was hesitant at first and looked into the puppet's plastic eyes for reassurance. But he eventually went along and found the elaborate story funny. Herbie had been on quite a journey. Jason was scheduled to pick up the boys for dinner again, so I called him to let him know the problem was solved.

When Jason arrived, Gavin ran across the front lawn with new Herbie in his hand. "Look, Daddy! Herbie is back!"

"Oh really, buddy?" Jason pulled the original Herbie from behind his back.

Gavin stopped short, bewildered. He didn't know what to believe. I had lied to him, and Jason was willing to hurt Gavin to hurt me. I shot Jason a look that could kill. He smirked and put the boys in his car. I was manic while they were at dinner. I had deceived Gavin, and I worried over how I would ever repair the damage. I shook with rage and paced around my house, recalling the mental games Jason had used to torture me and the boys over the years. My mind flooded with moments when the boys had come home reporting abuse I couldn't prevent, because the only solution seemed to be keeping them from Jason, but that would have meant risking more problems.

"Daddy spit on me," Ben told me after one visit. "He was

screaming at me, then he pulled me into a room by my arm and spit on me. He also calls me a punk and a son of a bitch."

"I told Daddy, 'Stop hurting my brother,'" Gavin explained. "But he called me a little shit and told me to mind my own business. I hide in my room when he's mean to Ben."

"We don't sleep with sheets on the beds at Daddy's house," they reported one night as I tucked them into their beds.

"Gavin sleeps in Tyler's room in the basement on a mattress on the floor. I sleep in the girls' room," Ben told me.

Gavin came home that night sad and confused.

"I called the family that found him," I told him. "They *thought* he was Herbie because he looked so much like him, but they made a mistake. Turns out it's Herbie's cousin," I said, laughing.

Gavin accepted my explanation and laughed a bit, but I could see the doubt in his eyes.

~

I tried to get help over the years, but it felt like there was no common sense in the world of family law. I called social services, wrote letters to the law guardian, and had the boys in therapy at times. Basically, Jason needed to be shooting heroin and beating the kids to a pulp in order for anyone to intervene. Otherwise, he had a right to see his children. Sometimes I'd get so angry, I'd pretend they were sick to give them a break from his abuse. It eventually backfired on me. The more I tried to keep him away from us, the more he made his presence known.

Jason coached Gavin's soccer team, and Ben was the mascot. Ben enjoyed cheering for the team and putting on halftime shows. One tournament weekend, Jason was handing out championship

T-shirts to the team. I don't know what happened on the side-lines during the games, but he was clearly furious with Ben. Jason made a grand display of handing out each boy's shirt like a rowdy announcer. Ben patiently waited for his name to be called. It wasn't.

"What about me?" he asked.

Jason ignored him, but I could see the tension in his face.

"What about me, Daddy?" Ben asked again.

Jason packed the ball bag and ignored him.

"C'mon, Ben," I called him over, trying to spare him any further hurt.

The boys and I walked toward my car. Jason hustled close behind. "You did great today, Gavin!" he said from right behind us. "I'm proud of you, buddy," he added.

"Can I have a shirt now, Daddy?" Ben wouldn't let it go. "You gave Gavin a shirt. Why not me?"

"Because I love Gavin more than I love you," Jason replied.

My insides burned. Ben began to cry. I scooped him up and fastened him in his booster seat. Gavin's eyes grew large. He jumped into the car and buckled himself in.

I sat in the driver's seat and looked at Ben in the rearview mirror. His chubby cheeks were soaked with tears.

"Ben, listen to me," I said, making eye contact with him in the mirror. "Listen to me good. There is *nothing* wrong with you, Ben. You hear me? *Nothing*." His eyes lit up. I had his full attention. "Daddy has a sickness. It's a sickness in the head. He probably needs medicine for it, but he doesn't take any. The sickness makes him do and say mean things. It's not your fault. There's *nothing* wrong with you."

Ben asked a few questions, intrigued by this sickness, and

seemed relieved to learn there was a reason for Jason's awful be-havior. I could have killed Jason that day. I recalled the words of the marriage counselor we had a few sessions with while we were separated. "Get yourself and your kids far away from this man," she advised. Instead, I kept the enemy close, believing I could rein in his malevolence.

"I asked Daddy why he doesn't take medicine," Ben told me after his next visit at Jason's.

Oh boy, I thought. "What did he say?" I asked.

"He didn't know what I was talking about. I told him you said he was sick in the head and needed medicine."

"He made us tell it on the video," Gavin chimed in.

This news alarmed me. "What video?"

"Daddy tapes us sometimes. He asks questions about you and about when Grandma babysits," Gavin explained.

I heard a ringing in my ears as my living room seemed to spin. My heart raced. I felt powerless to protect myself, so I pushed down thoughts that something sinister was at play, but thoughts of the video interrogations haunted me.

I was constantly thrown by Jason's ability to make me ques-tion reality. I started to wonder if Mom and I were behaving in a way that warranted interrogations. I tried to soothe my anxiety by inwardly discrediting him. I scoffed at his constant accusations of denied visits and the endless police presence at my home.

Jason had no problem missing visits with the kids when vis-its weren't convenient for him. In the span of a year, he traveled to Mexico, London, Germany, and Italy with friends or maybe his girlfriend. I received last-minute, vague details of these myste-rious trips, which of course meant he wouldn't be picking up the boys for his visitation days. He turned off his cell phone service, and we had no way to contact him during his trips. He came home demanding makeup times with the boys for "missed visits," as if I were the cause. When he did take the boys, he'd return them late, with no regard for school nights or my right to time, especially on holidays.

He had recently returned the boys a few hours late on Thanksgiving, and I anticipated he'd do the same on Christmas Eve.

"The agreement says you have the boys until 10:00 p.m.," I reminded him when he picked up Gavin and Ben that evening.

"Right," he replied noncommittally.

"I'll be out anyway, so I'll pick them up from you then," I offered, trying to be in control and make sure it happened.

He appeased me dismissively. "Sure."

After Jason picked up the boys, I drove to Brooklyn to meet my family at a restaurant. I was so wrapped up in my own dysfunction, I downplayed the dynamic in Theo's Greek family. He decided to spend the holidays with them without mentioning he had a girlfriend, because he knew they wouldn't accept a divorced mom, heaven forbid a non-Greek.

I was almost at the restaurant when my text alert chimed. "Negative on the pickup," was all it said.

I frantically called Jason. "The divorce agreement is clear. The boys are with you until 10:00 p.m. on Christmas Eve. I'll pick them up then," I insisted.

"They're with me for the school break this week," he said. "I don't need to follow the Christmas Eve language. I'll make sure you have your time with them tomorrow. Now please try to calm down and enjoy your holidays," he said in a patronizing tone. "The boys are having a great time with me and Dottie and the kids."

"Jason, I'm picking them up at 10:00 p.m.!" I screamed.

He hung up.

I turned the car around, called my parents to explain why I wouldn't be at dinner, and drove to the police station, where I begged for help as if my children had been kidnapped. The thought of not being with them when they woke up to Santa's presents in the morning was like a kick in the gut. Jason was threatening my connection with my kids. I was in a panic that their childhood was being robbed from me and that we would be forever damaged from the broken Christmas morning. I needed them home. I needed our bond and traditions and joy to be intact.

The police officers empathized, but unless the boys were in danger, they couldn't remove them from Jason's custody. They wrote a report that I would have to take up in family court. I walked out of the precinct in a trance, feeling like I'd just been through a tragedy. My anxiety ramped up as my mind spun countless irrational worst-case scenarios. I feared Jason would kidnap the boys. I spent most of the night on the phone with my mom and my friend Kristine, ranting about how awful he was.

～

The next morning, I parked outside his house, called his cell phone, and demanded the boys.

"They're opening a few more gifts." Jason sounded chipper. "They'll be out shortly."

My heart swelled with relief when Gavin and Ben emerged from Jason's broken screen door. When my fear subsided, anger roared.

"Your father was supposed to bring you home last night," I said as soon as they hopped in the car. "Santa came, and all your gifts have been waiting for you." I was fuming.

"Daddy said you called and said you weren't going to be home last night. He said you told him you would just see us in the morning," Gavin nervously explained.

"Mommy would never cancel on you." I fought to cover my rage at Jason's lies. "Daddy made that up."

"He says you're mean. When you call him his phone plays, 'You're a Mean One, Mr. Grinch,'" Ben said.

I bit back a snippy retort. "That's not very nice," I said.

I tried changing the subject to defuse the tension. "What did Santa bring you at Daddy's?"

"Santa doesn't come to Dad's house. Dad buys all the gifts there. Santa just comes to our house," Gavin explained. Jason refused to be second, even to Santa.

~

My family came over that afternoon and filled my living room with gifts and anger. In between spoiling the boys, they fed my fury about the night before. I wanted to calm down, but I couldn't around them.

"That fat bastard," my mother said all day.

My father spewed empty threats. "I'll break his legs."

Merry Christmas, I thought.

chapter fifteen

JASON WAS SUPPOSED TO PICK THE BOYS UP FOR THE REST OF the school break week, but to punish him, I told him they were sick and couldn't go. He parked outside my house every day, beeping and ringing the bell.

"Go away! The boys aren't feeling well!" I yelled from the window, fueled by my need for revenge. I was too angry to realize I was playing right into his plan. Police cars eventually pulled up and rang my bell, because Jason expressed concern for the boys' well-being, alleging he hadn't heard from us for days. I spent the week twisted with anger, anxiety, and frustration.

~

I decided to move. I regretted buying Jason out and staying in the house we'd bought while married. I convinced myself that selling the house would set me free. The FOR SALE sign on my front lawn made me feel powerful. Little did I know there was a much larger power at play.

Almost three years after we'd settled the divorce, my doorbell rang, followed by aggressive pounding on the door. I recognized that knocking the way a soldier recognizes the sound of gunfire. It instantly transported me back to when I was served with divorce papers.

The past few years flashed before my eyes. Jason had been trying to punish me ever since I ended the marriage. He didn't want me back; he wanted to get back *at* me. He turned everyday life into a series of domestic-incident reports, his allegations coming up just short of abduction. There was a constant police presence at my home.

Email became another tool for torture. He flooded my inbox with false accusations meant to incite my fury. My responses were less than poetic, oftentimes crazed. His nonstop harassment made me nuts.

One of his favorite strategies was to return the boys home hours late after weekend visits, filthy, without shoes and jackets, tired and hungry. Their condition deteriorated with each Sunday evening drop-off. At times, I responded in a fit of rage and did not make the boys available for an upcoming visit. I foolishly thought I was establishing a boundary. Instead, I reacted exactly as he hoped, giving him the ammunition he needed.

Now here was that all-too-familiar, ominous drumming on the door. I peered out a window. Sure enough, what appeared to be an ex-con was standing on our doorstep clutching a fistful of papers. I tried to ignore the banging, as if I could pretend this chaos out of my life. But at almost six and seven, the boys were still little. They grew frightened as the thuds continued. When I opened the door, the thug looked at me as if I deserved to suffer and he enjoyed being the one to inflict the pain.

Accepting the papers triggered a profound sense of shame.

"Mommy, who was that guy?" Gavin asked. "What did he give you?"

My head was spinning as I fought to craft a lie. "Oh, just some angry neighbor trying to get us all to sign a petition to have the streets paved. Don't worry," I reassured him with feigned nonchalance.

I read the papers with shaking hands. I was trying to act strong in an effort to convince myself as well as the kids that I was okay, but I was petrified. This was far bigger than a routine court proceeding. Jason was suing me for full custody of the boys under the grounds of parental alienation. His two-sentence petition alleged he was being denied contact with his sons. He lived three blocks away from us, exercised regular dinner and weekend visitation, coached their teams, and attended all school functions. I even gave him extra time with the boys to help cover my work schedule. The accusation was based on the strategically crafted, self-serving paper trail he had fabricated with emails and police reports. This made it even more frightening.

The petition was preposterous. I tried not to take it seriously. My mind searched for stories to counter my fear, which quickly turned into blame. I blamed my ex; I blamed the court system. The boys were healthy, happy, well cared for, and loved. I had full custody, and they had regular contact with their dad. Custody battles were for celebrities or addicts or abusers, not loving, attentive mothers.

I paced from room to room, tidying up, while panic raced through me. I was desperate for it to stop, desperate for someone to help me, and afraid of how alone I was. I downplayed Jason's presence in my life to Theo, sharing only glimpses of our contentious relationship. I needed to pull myself together for the boys.

"C'mon, guys, hop in the bath!" I yelled. I ran the bath and added extra bubbles. The boys splashed and played while I smiled and tried to be present. But my mind was playing out a scene far different from the one in front of me. I was sure Jason didn't really want custody. It would turn his world upside down. He was probably out at a bar watching a game or sitting around a poker table in someone's basement with a cigar in his hand while I was doing bath time after a long day at work. The petition wasn't about our kids. It was about his desire to punish me. He needed to destroy me. He needed to win.

Ten days later, Jason withdrew his petition for custody. I was relieved at first, but as I crossed the court appearance off my calendar, I couldn't shake the sense that it wasn't finished. Jason would never let me off that easily.

~

One morning a couple of weeks later, I hurried the boys out the mudroom door and walked toward my car, feeling proud of how I had it all together with plenty of time to drop the kids at school and make the train to the city. When I reached the car, a burly guy dressed from head to toe in denim and smelling of cigarette smoke shoved some papers at my chest. I let them fall to my feet while I hurried the boys into their booster seats. I buckled them up in a frenzy, trying to pretend nothing had happened, but my hands shook.

"Who was that guy, Mommy?" Gavin asked. "Why did he throw that envelope at you?"

I knew better than to bad-mouth my ex to our children, but my panic and rage got the best of me. "Your father is taking me to court, because he wants to take you guys away from me. He doesn't want you to live with Mommy. He wants you to live at his house." Inwardly I cringed as I chipped away at their childhood innocence.

The boys' eyes grew large with confusion and alarm. "Why?" asked Gavin.

"We don't want to live at his house!" Ben exclaimed.

"We want to live with you," added Gavin.

Guilt and fear stymied my efforts to reassure them that nothing was going to happen. I dropped them off at school, leaving them no choice but to follow my lead and push their fears down and go about their day.

I sat on the train and read the same custody petition that claimed parental alienation and denied access to the children. I'd been married to Jason for four years and endured over two years of divorce proceedings, plus a few years coexisting under the terms of our settlement—more than long enough to know his dark side. He was planning something sinister.

I would need an attorney again. I frantically contemplated how I would pay for this round. I'd spent over $100,000 in attorneys' fees during our divorce. I could do a cash-back refinance on the house, or use credit card checks from the high interest rate offers I received in the mail, or sell jewelry, or borrow from my parents—again. I was constantly choosing between financial ruin and codependency. I went through the day distracted, scared, and angry, doing my best to hide my dysfunctional personal life from my boss and coworkers.

Theo had been itching to buy a place after renting an apartment for years. We discussed a future together, but he wasn't ready to fully commit. He dreaded his family's reaction, he questioned the responsibility of children who weren't his own, and he was skeptical about the dynamic with Jason. His reservations added to my insecurities, and I began exhausting myself to please him. The more desperate I grew, the more distant he seemed.

Fearing my life was getting stale, a sense of urgency to shake things up pushed me to act on my own. I started looking for my own house. I thought it was a sign of strength and independence, a way to show Theo I wasn't waiting for him.

When it came time to actually buy a new place, I got caught up in fear, mommy guilt, and the *Moron Manual*. My dream of living in the city seemed out of reach. I believed the boys were too settled in suburban living. I searched only as far as other Prospect Isle towns but still gravitated toward our current one. I didn't want the boys to have the burden of separate lives between houses.

Deep down, I needed to keep the distance between our home and Jason's short enough so I could control and manage their visits and protect them from any harm. I had so many fear-based issues that I rationalized as sound decision-making. My mom fed my fear by letting me know her limits on how far she'd travel to babysit. I didn't realize the toll it was all taking on her.

With Jason's petition for custody hanging over my head, I went into contract on a house only a few blocks from my current one. I believed this would placate Jason and get him to back off. I relied on the new house to create boundaries I didn't know how to establish.

I continued to go about my business as if the drama in my life was a subplot. After the papers were served, I still went to work, and the boys went to school. We attended a birthday party at a bounce house place, we ordered pizza, and we went to basketball practice. I took out the garbage, chatted on the phone, and went to the playground with the neighbors. The boys laughed and played and argued and ran through the house like any other brothers. I wonder if they recall those days with fondness or if their memories are tainted with awareness of their mother's anxiety. I know painfully well that we will never get that time in our lives back.

~

On the morning of my court appearance, I put the boys on the school bus, grabbed a coffee, and drove to family court. I called my friend Kristine and ranted as I drove.

"Can you believe I have to deal with this crap? He's obsessed with torturing me. He has nothing better to do with his life. His mother is probably egging him on. They get their thrills from messing with my life. I had to take off work for this nonsense. He doesn't have to worry about missing a day at his job. He didn't have to get the kids off to school before racing over to court." I was afraid of my fear; anger seemed to serve me better.

I hung up the phone and combed the courthouse parking lot for a spot, but it was full. I frantically searched for parking, fighting the urge to drive away.

In the courthouse, I waited in line to go through the metal detectors while all the attorneys flashed their badges and walked through their special entrance. I felt unworthy, judged, and rejected. There was an innocent young girl, full of light and joy, somewhere deep inside of me, but the two separate entrances spoke volumes. I was damaged. This stung to the core. I felt ashamed as I stripped all of my personal belongings into a bin to be scanned by the court officers.

Inside, the halls were dingy. It felt more like a detention facility than a courthouse. Women stood in line waiting to file petitions for child support or orders of protection. Some had babies on their hips or in strollers. Couples screamed and cursed at one another while court-appointed mediators and attorneys tried to reason with them. Teenagers escorted by social workers waited to hear their fate after their latest juvenile detention stays. Judges and law guardians were paged on the loudspeakers. I signed in and then sat in the holding room waiting for Stuart, my attorney, to arrive.

Cases were called.

"Parties on *Smith v. Smith* to Judge Warner."

"Parties on *Jones v. Jones* to Judge Ellias."

Your family name echoed down a hallway, and you had to jump.

Stuart finally appeared. He was young and inexperienced, but I'd hired him because he was inexpensive. At almost thirty-six years old, hiring my own attorney without the help of my parents gave me a sense of control over my life. During our initial consultation, he had assured me that the matter would be handled as easily as a traffic violation.

Jason arrived in his navy-blue suit, shiny shoes, and cunning smirk. He paced the halls as if he couldn't wait to get in front of the judge. He actually seemed excited by the whole thing. I simultaneously wanted to kill him and beg him for mercy. He had me pinned, the same way he had pinned me to the wall at the hotel in Disney.

Jason's crony and attorney, Nick Napolitano, was with him for the hearing. Nick was the ultimate politician, always smiling for a photo opportunity in the local papers. He fixed streets, planted trees, and volunteered at schools. He attended the local church, sat on every committee in town, and acted like everyone's best friend.

"Parties on *Axcel v. Miracola*." The announcement signaled doom. I was at the mercy of strangers who would decide my fate, and worse, the fate of my children. I filed into a small makeshift courtroom along with Stuart; my ex-husband and his pal Nick; and Abe Gladstone, the law guardian from our divorce proceedings assigned to represent the children.

We were before Referee Abruzzi, a mousy-looking young punk who used his position to compensate for his lack of height. Referees, or junior judges, were allowed to hear custody matters in New York. He entered the room from a back door, gently swinging his cape as if Batman had arrived. But he was no hero. He ordered us to be seated as he reigned high above the parties he was there to judge.

Criminal attorneys get to screen jurors, but my attorney had no say in picking the referee. I later learned Abruzzi had gone through a bitter divorce and custody battle himself. I was stuck with a jaded creep with the power to make life-changing decisions for my family and me. My chances would have been better had I committed murder.

Abruzzi was jumpy as he flipped through our file. His movements mimicked a boxer in the corner of the ring, waiting for the bell. He sized up the room, sympathetically nodding at my ex, indicating they were in the same corner. He shifted his attention toward me and scowled. He stared at me, but he did not see me. I was never going to be able to connect with the guy.

I looked around the room, desperate for someone to take all the power and control away from these domineering men. No one else seemed panicked. No one else seemed to sense the magnitude of the drama that was at play. I gasped for air while everyone else breathed freely. I made eye contact with the court stenographer. Her tired eyes said, "Sorry, honey. I just type the notes and collect my check. There's nothing I can do for you."

We stated our names and addresses for the record. I had no choice but to follow the process, even though I was losing myself and my children. I felt their little hands slipping from mine, and suddenly I had a savage desire to save us all from irreparable harm. My lawyer should have asked for an immediate dismissal of the petition, as it was deficient as a matter of law. But I'd hired a young and basically clueless attorney, hoping my denial of the situation would make it go away. It didn't. That was the spring of 2007. I didn't breathe again until the fall of 2010.

chapter sixteen

custody, I moved into my new home. And then found out I was pregnant. It was as if I were living a real-life version of the *Choose Your Own Adventure* books I had read as a child.

Theo panicked at first. He'd recently told his family about me. In response, they tried to set him up with single Greek girls from his mom's church. His sister treated me like a second- class citizen. Her harsh judgment and narrow-minded beliefs made the *Moron Manual* seem permissive. Despite tremendous pressure from his family to break up with me, he committed to our baby and me, and moved in with me and the boys. When he shared the news of the pregnancy with his family, they shifted their energies toward making me Greek. They offered the right dose of hysteria and absurdity to distract me from the custody battle with Jason.

Theo pulled up to my house with his U-Haul, and I felt like my knight in shining armor had arrived. I deluded myself into thinking Jason would fade away while Theo and the boys and I lived the utopian dream. But the knot in my stomach reminded me it was self-deception. I didn't want to live in the new house in the same neighborhood. I felt Jason's presence like a dark cloud over me, and I felt guilty for sucking Theo into my world. Anxious that I'd made more of a mess, I scurried about trying to make sure Theo was happy and the boys accepted him. I was a nervous wreck whenever they had a hard time adjusting to living together. I absorbed everyone's upsets and dizzied myself trying to manage their emotions. I held my hand over my belly to protect the baby from my stress.

Chills ran up my spine every time Jason came to pick up the boys, especially when it was for longer than a quick dinner. The divorce agreement allowed him two nonconsecutive summer weeks with them. My heart was heavy as I packed up their things for their first week with him that July. At just six and seven, they seemed too little to leave Mommy for so long.

"High five, kiss, and a hug," I said to Gavin at the door.

"High five, kiss, and a hug," he replied.

I slapped his hand, kissed the top of his baseball cap, and hugged him tight. His zest for life and enthusiasm for play warmed my heart. He walked toward Jason's car, down for whatever was planned for the week, looking for a good time. I mistook his optimism and adaptability for naivete and feared he'd be easily influenced by Jason's manipulative ways. I grew overprotective, always trying to get ahead of perceived threats to Gavin's well-being, dreading the world would steal his spirit the way it stole mine.

"High five, kiss, and a hug," I said to Ben.

"High five, kiss, and a hug," he replied without his brother's enthusiasm.

He clenched his blankie and showed me his half of the secret note we'd written to each other. It was a paper heart, cut in half, with messages meant to comfort each other while we were apart. I needed my half as much as he needed his. My heart warmed at his bravery as he walked down the driveway toward Jason's car, toward the father who'd spit on him.

"Want to grab dinner?" Theo asked when I stepped back inside. He had no way to know the depth of my pain.

"I just want to go for a walk," I replied. I laced up my sneakers, drove to the high school track, and walked a few laps in tears. I used to walk a lot with my mom around a track when I lived at home in Queens. I wanted to call her to vent, but she wasn't as sharp as she used to be. We'd recently learned she had early onset Alzheimer's, but I couldn't grasp the diagnosis. I didn't know how to relate to the dwindling version of her, and I was angry at her for changing. I was slowly losing my mom while Jason was trying to take my boys from me. But I prided myself on my resilience and refused to let life get the best of me. I wiped my eyes, pulled myself together, and went home to Theo.

We grabbed a bite and spent the "free" week setting up our shared home, but I was totally checked out. I felt bad about not being fully available to Theo after how much his life had recently changed for me. It must have been hard enough for him to leave his bachelor pad at almost forty, break the Greek code, take on two stepsons and a puppy, and endure a long commute to his office. Jason was the icing on the cake. I found myself acquiescing to traditional expectations that were ingrained in him and agreeing to his every decision, partly out of guilt and partly because I didn't have the energy to do otherwise. He imposed the strict, rigid ways of his Orthodox childhood on the free-spirited home I had created with my boys. He watched *Supernanny* religiously and tried to implement her suggestions, negating my instincts for a more easygoing style. I agreed to baptize the baby in the Greek Orthodox Church instead of my church, thinking it didn't matter anyway. Nothing mattered anymore. I even hated all the furniture he chose, but I was too unnerved to speak up.

~

I waited patiently at my front door for the boys to return home Friday evening. It started getting late, and I feared Jason wasn't bringing them home. I called him to check on the timing.

"Hello?" He sounded chipper.

"What time are you dropping off the boys? I'm waiting for them for dinner." My snippy tone wouldn't get him to oblige, and I was making a fool of myself trying.

"I'll have them home to you Sunday night," he assured me.

"Sunday night? It's my weekend!" I exclaimed.

"It's my vacation week," he clarified.

"You picked them up last Friday. It's been a week already. It's my weekend with them now," I said.

"Fran, I'm not going to have this debate with you now. I'm away with Dottie and the kids. We plan to drive back Sunday. Goodbye." He hung up.

Jason had come up with a clever plan to *start* his vacation week at the *end* of his weekend and keep the boys right through my weekend. Doing that once in July and once in August left me with only one weekend for each month. Even though I had full custody, it felt like I was the weekday nanny, with limited summer family time.

I paced my den, phone in hand, wondering what to do. I called my attorney, but he was gone for the day. I tried my friend Kristine, but she was busy with her kids and told me to enjoy the free time. Instead, I spent the weekend on the phone complaining to any friend that would listen and sitting around with my arms folded, waiting for the boys to come home. I watched Theo putter around the house, oblivious to my anguish.

Sunday night finally came, and the boys ran toward my front door with smiles on their faces, happy to be home. I wanted to hug them and shower them with love, but I couldn't see past my hatred for Jason. I'd waited ten days to see them, and when I finally did, my head spun like I was possessed.

"You were supposed to be home Friday night," I complained. Their smiles dimmed. "We missed a whole weekend together, and now I have to work tomorrow," I whined.

They looked at me with puppy eyes.

"I told Dad you thought we were coming home Friday, but he said that wasn't true," Gavin explained. "I can't make him drive us home," he said, frustrated to be in the middle.

"Dottie even tried to leave him with her kids, but he wouldn't let her go," Ben added.

Unreal, I thought, frustrated that Jason sold himself as Mr. Family Guy while his new wife was trying to escape.

"They had a brawl," Ben went on while Gavin went to play his video games.

I was angry at myself for letting Jason get the best of me and for acting up in front of my boys.

Don't give him the satisfaction. I could hear my mom's voice in my head. I booked a quick family vacation at an all-inclusive resort for a few days. We came home to a family court petition and a police report alleging I had denied Jason access to his children, because he'd missed a weekday dinner while we were away. Technically, there was no specific mention in our divorce settlement of me having vacation time with the boys. But there was no need to spell it out; I had full custody, so it was implied. But Jason seemed to think I wasn't entitled to a vacation. My chest burned with rage at his twisted interpretation.

Furious, and adamant about not giving Jason power over me, I called my attorney and told him I wasn't going to the next court appearance. I told Stuart to go alone and represent me. "Tell them I'm pregnant and it's high risk," I ordered. At my last doctor's appointment, I'd learned there was a deficiency with the umbilical cord. I would need frequent sonograms and close monitoring. I had the baby to think about. I found strength in my role as a mother and decided to go about my life with my growing family as if Jason was not a factor.

I blew off court as planned, refusing to give it or Jason any credibility. I convinced myself that Stuart and the law guardian would swiftly resolve Jason's matter of denied access to the boys and the case would be dismissed.

My cell phone rang late that afternoon.

Stuart scolded me. "The referee didn't appreciate you not showing up. He ordered that for the next three weekends, the boys will be with your ex to make up for his missed visits," he explained.

"Missed visits?!" I was stunned. "Jason had more time with them this summer than I did!" I reminded him. "Did you explain how Jason manipulated summer vacation language to take away *my* weekends? Did you explain that when I go away for a few days, Jason cries 'missed visits'?" I was so sick of spelling it all out.

"I did."

"What the hell did the law guardian have to say?" I asked.

He regurgitated the common sense I knew. "He agreed that Dad shouldn't expand his week into Mom's weekends and that Mom should have uninterrupted vacation time as well."

"And?" I asked, sharp-tongued.

"The referee still did what he did. I'll send you a copy of the order." It was regrettable but done. Beyond the blow to his lawyering skills, the order wasn't Stuart's problem.

Why was I at the mercy of Jason and court? *Hell no*, something inside me roared. I held my hand over my belly. *I'm the mother.*

I blamed Stuart for being an idiot and dismissed Jason's and the referee's power over me. I made a few calls and was referred to a powerhouse attorney, Barry Nagel. We had a brief phone consultation. I quickly filled him in, barely taking a breath. He earnestly took my side, reacting at the right trigger points. He assured me he could help and would be happy to take the case. I let out a sigh of relief that finally someone got it and would save me. I just had to meet him at his office to formally retain him and pay a $20,000 retainer. I cringed. This saga wasn't going to go over well with Theo, who was extremely frugal with finances. He grew up with an immigrant fear that money would run out. Meanwhile, Jason's buddy was representing him pro bono. None of this was fair.

~

Jason pulled up with his dad to pick up the boys for the first of his additional weekends. "Hey, buddies!" he called out. "Ready for a fun weekend with Daddy?" he shouted, making a display of his time with the boys for the neighbors.

"Come give Pop-Pop a hug," Bob chimed in. He hugged the boys and patted Jason on the back as they walked toward the car. *Spineless traitor,* I thought as I recalled the times he'd visited behind Jason's back.

"Hop in, boys. Dottie, the kids, and Nana are waiting for us at the house," Jason bellowed as he smiled at me. My body tensed with frustration. I shot hateful daggers through him with my eyes. He smirked, unaffected. I hated myself for being his victim.

Charged with energy to get control, I went into my den. I stared at my calendar, trying to wrap my head around how bad this temporary order was. The visual of my planner always soothed me. My cousin's baby's baptism fell on an upcoming weekend that would have been mine if not for Jason and the damn referee. Later that week, I emailed Jason. Like a prisoner begging for privileges, I begged for time with my boys: "Jason, I know you have the boys again next weekend, but I was planning to take them to my cousin's party. Can we work out arrangements for me to have them for a few hours to attend?"

I lost all dignity as I hit send.

His reply stung: "Unfortunately, Dottie and I have plans with the kids next weekend. I know this new schedule will take some getting used to."

My insides burned. His gloating tormented me more than his abuse. Rage boiled in me, and I grew wild under his power, unable to free myself from his grasp. He pushed without limits, hoping to break me.

"Makeup" weekends and self-appointed extended summer vacations weren't enough for him. He signed up to serve lunch at the elementary school with the PTA moms. He charmed and dazzled them, complimenting their haircuts and weight loss. No one questioned how he had so much time off from work, even though their taxpayer dollars were paying his town salary. He called the principal's office to request second mailings of all school notices as well as separate time slots for parent teacher conferences. Meanwhile, he never even opened a book with the boys. He scheduled all practices for teams he coached during my dinner evenings. He handed me a monthly child support check in front of other parents instead of mailing it to me.

Other families in the neighborhood learned Jason was suing me for full custody. I sensed some were questioning my decency while empathizing with his pursuit. He had them convinced he was a devoted father, desperate for time with his boys. I felt like I was going mad. I loathed them for their judgment and was shocked by the audacity of their gossip about me and worse, my boys. One day after school, some moms gathered at the playground to chitchat while the kids played kickball on the field. A commotion erupted over a play. Gavin thought he was safe, while another boy called him out at the plate. The majority sided with Gavin and his run count. The boy kicked dirt toward Gavin.

"My run's gonna be the game winner," Gavin said mockingly.

"At least my parents aren't divorced," the other boy taunted with a venom he had learned from an adult.

Countless times over the years, people made derogatory comments about children of divorced families. I so badly wanted to tell people that their behind-closed-doors dysfunction was far worse than my divorce. I wanted to plow through suburbia with a hatchet, chopping at people who had nothing better to do than threaten my family.

Jason, on the other hand, had no shame and no problem using the boys in his needling games against me. Gavin came home after another weekend at Jason's, the front of his jet-black hair bleached blonde. He anxiously looked up at me, anticipating my reaction.

I overreacted as a result of ongoing irritation. "What happened to your hair?"

"Miss Dottie did it." He probably thought she was less of a trigger for me than his dad. "Do you like it?" he sheepishly asked.

"No, Gavin. It's trash!" I exclaimed. "You look like her trash family." *Who the hell was she to dye his hair?*

I was mortified at the thought of Gavin going to school like that. I was already judged, now this. I had Theo buzz Gavin's head, military style. I refused to allow Jason to blemish my image.

The next weekend was finally mine. I walked Gavin toward the soccer field, and Jason flashed a satisfied smile.

"Why'd you cut your hair, buddy?" he asked.

"Mom didn't like the blonde," Gavin replied.

"She didn't, huh?" He smirked. "Next time I'll give you a mohawk."

I shot Jason a look of disgust. I looked over at his now purple-haired girlfriend, standing with Joanne, who was wearing a fur coat over a blue sweat suit. I rolled my eyes with haughty disdain, as if I could snub them out of my life. But I couldn't, and I could tell Jason knew he was getting to me. And I knew from experience that meant he would up the ante.

chapter seventeen

I PEERED OUT THE WINDOW AND SAW BOB HOLDING A VIDEO camera while Jason waited on my front lawn to pick up the boys. Bob was so desperate for a relationship with his surviving son, he'd do anything to buddy up with him. I presumed they were hoping to catch me acting out. Where was he planning to play these videos, I wondered? What could they possibly reveal?

I grew paranoid. Everyone was watching me; everyone was judging me. Part of the custody battle included a court-ordered forensic evaluation—an in-depth psychological analysis of each parent and members of the family in order to determine the best interest of the children. The referee assigned Dr. David Levine to our case. His practice was in town, and I'd considered using Levine when I was looking for a therapist for Ben. We didn't get further than a consultation, because he wouldn't take our insurance. The forensics assignment wasn't a bad gig; Levine earned about $15,000 to analyze, judge, and issue a report with his recommendations.

The day of my first appointment, I sat in Levine's waiting room, flipping through a magazine, my leg jiggling. Dr. Levine's office door opened, and he walked out with his arm on the back of an adolescent boy. The boy stared down at his sneakers while Dr. Levine quickly addressed his mom. "Same time next week?" he asked.

"Yes, thank you, Doctor," she meekly replied. *Who the hell was this guy to tell you what's best for your son?* I thought. *Get yourself together, woman,* I wanted to scream.

"Mrs. Axcel." He looked at me. I hated being referred to by my marital name.

"Yes." I straightened up, too obedient to correct him, waiting for him to tell me it was okay to stand and follow him.

I sat on the couch along the wall, across from his sovereign chair. His office was filled with books to convey his intelligence. Certificates hung on the wall to display his credibility. He knew better than me, his office screamed. I was a little girl who needed scolding and schooling.

He made some pleasant small talk, but I wasn't relaxed. He finally leaned forward to turn on his mini recorder. He leaned back, crossed his legs, and cradled a notebook and a pen. He wasn't there to help; he was there to judge.

At the end of the introductory meeting, he explained the rest of the process. I needed to schedule the psychological exams during the week while he was in with his regular patients. He conducted his forensics sessions between 7:00 and 8:00 a.m. on Saturdays. I had to drag my pregnant self out of bed, sometimes with the boys, for multiple sessions over the next few months.

Jason was subjected to the same process, although I speculated that he approached his sessions eagerly. He had the audacity to ask me to pack nice clothes on his weekends so the boys would look presentable on his Saturdays at Levine's.

One Saturday, we all met together. Jason put on the ultimate family guy show, but his evident hatred for me made his performance unconvincing. His acting was so fake, even the boys seemed repelled. Ben sat on my lap, and Gavin snuggled up against me.

They were too honest to relate to Jason's phoniness. I thought for sure Levine would pick up on the fact that Jason's behavior was off, rehearsed.

The doctor met with Theo, Dottie, my parents, and Jason's parents. My parents and Theo were coached by my attorney as if they were witnesses being called in a murder trial. It was too much for my mother to bear. Signs of dementia were setting in; my dad said she couldn't even tell Levine how old she was. My father, on the other hand, was confident he'd charmed the doctor. Theo cooperated fully and stood by me. I felt guilty watching him get ready early Saturday mornings for his appointments.

Test days were in a small, all-white room with a window covered by tightly shut blinds. I was aware that right outside was a restaurant where other moms met for lunch, and down the street was the nursery school the boys had attended. Suburban life was going on outside while I was in what felt like a padded room, taking tests. There was something very wrong with how I existed. But when I picked up the pencil, I transformed into a young girl as I filled in little circles, hoping to get 100 percent like I used to in school. I was excited there was an essay section, which I usually excelled in. I reviewed the booklet before handing it in, hoping the doctor would be impressed with me. I suddenly realized it was ridiculous of me to be playing the role of a good student. It was strange how much I was able to block out and normalize. It felt like I had power, but I sensed it wasn't serving me.

One Saturday morning, I sat on Levine's couch, exhausted. Levine and I barely exchanged hellos as he leaned forward to hit the record button.

"Jason mentioned you told Ben he was sick in the head?" Levine started.

I sighed with frustration at the context in which the story must have been relayed. I confidently filled Levine in, certain he would understand I was trying to protect Ben from Jason's abuse. He stared blankly at me, nodded, and jotted down some notes.

I shared stories of my own, nervously trying to get Levine to grasp what I dealt with, convinced anyone with half a brain would get it. I even told him about Herbie the hand puppet to drive home the point that I tried to co-parent with Jason, but he made it impossible. Even worse, I said, he used the boys in his battles with me. I told him Jason conducted video interrogations of the boys. The more I shared, the more obvious my plight became. But Levine didn't seem to register any of it. He showed no compassion, and his process seemed to lack common sense.

"I don't like that guy," Ben said after a session. He was a very intuitive kid.

"Why, baby?" I asked, needing him to validate my gut feelings.

"He's a fake," Ben said, unwavering.

I drove home in silence, sensing something ominous on the horizon.

~

After my final appointment with the boys, Levine seemed to warm up for a minute. He rubbed Gavin on the head as we walked out the door. "He's such a great boy," Levine said to me. "And so handsome, too," he added. "You must be proud to have him as a son."

I smiled, sensing something was not right. His strong interest in Gavin creeped me out, and his conspicuous exclusion of

Ben raised a red flag. I couldn't tell if he was a pervert or if he was trying to prompt me to talk about Ben. I stared mutely and ushered my boys out the door.

The following weekend, my doorbell rang. I was shocked to see Dr. Levine at the door with a clipboard in his hand. I couldn't imagine what he wanted.

"Good morning. I need to inspect both parents' homes to finalize my review," he explained. "May I come in?"

It was a rhetorical question. He walked right by me into my living room. I followed him around as he walked through our bedrooms and bathrooms and even opened our medicine cabinet, taking notes along the way. I was thankful there was a picture of Jason and the boys in their room. I had to score major points with that, I thought. I cringed at the beer bottle Theo had left in the sink the night before, as if a grown man having a beer was a scandal. I wondered what Levine thought of the laundry basket in the hall.

"Thank you. That'll be all," he said as he walked toward the door.

I smiled like a deer in headlights as I let him out.

It wasn't easy to be a mom at risk of losing her children while working, pregnant, blending Theo and the boys under one roof, and watching my mom fade away. I persevered, as if surviving was a sign of strength. But I knew real strength wasn't about how I suffered through circumstances. I wanted to command my own life, but I just couldn't figure out how to do so. Instead, I played by the rules and burned with resentment. Like a fool, I paid an exorbitant amount of money along the way. My annual bonus went to Levine's fee and Barry's retainer.

chapter eighteen

I COULD NOT BELIEVE I WAS SITTING IN FAMILY COURT WAITING for my obstetrician to testify about my pregnancy. Jason gleefully paced the halls, rubbing his hands together and laughing with Nick. The doctor sat alone. He was there for me but not part of my team. He looked at me with the same confusion and concern that I'd seen many times before. Barry spoke to him briefly before an angry court employee shouted our names, and we scurried into Referee Abruzzi's tiny room.

Even Barry seemed on edge. He had reviewed my file when I retained him, but he couldn't make sense of how things had played out to date. Why did Jason file for custody, withdraw, then file again? He suspected Jason had gone forum shopping, which I learned meant trying to get the case in front of a particular judge. Barry sensed things were inexplicably looking pretty bad for me, and he wanted to delay the trial to buy himself time to prepare. I hoped time would magically make it go away. Barry had me ask my obstetrician to sign an affidavit that I was in the midst of a high-risk pregnancy and shouldn't be put under undo stress. It made me cringe to ask, but I'd grown accustomed to asking for humiliating help. Levine required letters from friends and community members describing me as a person and a mother. I had to ask the pediatrician to fill out a questionnaire for the forensics review. I needed copies of school records from the main office at our elementary school for Levine's files. The obstetrician signed the affidavit, and Barry submitted a motion asking for a temporary adjournment of the upcoming trial to March 2008, a couple of months after the baby was due.

Referee Abruzzi refused to honor the letter from the doctor and instead subpoenaed the obstetrician to appear in family court to testify under oath. We were all called to a hearing. The law guardian replied that he wasn't available; I wondered if he simply refused to participate in the nonsense. It was determined on the record that his presence wasn't necessary, because no decisions regarding custody or visitation were before the court that day. The hearing was simply to determine whether or not the trial needed to be temporarily adjourned.

I hated having to rise before Referee Abruzzi. My maternity dress and protruding belly stood out among the dark suits worn by all the men. I once again glanced at the court stenographer. She seemed even more beaten down by life than I was.

"Doctor, can you please describe the defendant's condition?" asked Abruzzi after my obstetrician was on the witness stand.

"Sure. There's a deficiency in the umbilical cord. Only two vessels are present instead of the typical three," the doctor explained.

"And what are the risks associated with a deficient umbilical cord?" Abruzzi questioned.

"There's a risk that the fetus is not getting enough nutrients. If the baby isn't growing properly during the last trimester, we might make the decision to deliver early to provide nutrients outside the womb."

My face burned red with embarrassment. I felt like I was lying on an exam table with my legs in the stirrups in front of all the men in the room.

"If we provide frequent breaks during the trial for drinks and snacks, would the defendant be able to proceed?" the referee pushed, as if he'd come up with a brilliant solution.

The doctor frowned. "I wouldn't recommend that. The stress of the trial and the physical strain on the mother could be a detriment to the fetus."

"So the mother shouldn't incur any physical activity?" he prodded. "Is she unable to take care of her two children at home?" My heart rate went through the roof as the referee exposed his punitive desires.

"She can take care of her children and go about her daily routine." The doctor seemed annoyed at the line of questioning. "I do not recommend the added burden of this setting, mentally and physically," he added as he scanned the room.

"Thank you. That's all." Abruzzi was done.

The doctor looked at me and Barry, hopeful that he'd done what he could to spare me from this insanity. We were all dismissed, and Jason nodded at the referee like he was bowing before his god. He chuckled loudly as he walked down the hall with his buddy Nick, patting him on the back. Barry and I thanked the doctor. I was touched by his kindness and felt so bad that he'd taken the time out of his schedule to be there.

Barry and I lingered in a dingy hallway. "What do you think?" I desperately asked.

"He'll have to grant the adjournment after that testimony," Barry assured me. "There's no way he can move forward with trial while you're carrying the baby."

"That's good," I said, but I sensed Barry's uncertainty.

"I'm just not sure what else this prick will do going forward." He rubbed his beard. "Snacks and water—the nerve," he added.

~

Gavin had a flag football game the weekend after the hearing. He loved flag football and played each game like it was Super Bowl Sunday. I sat quietly on the sidelines while Jason's entourage—Joanne, Bob, Dottie, and her three kids—loudly made their presence known. Ben played alongside my chair, always in a world of imagination.

After the game, Jason did his usual ritual of recapping plays with Gavin, offering excessive praise and overbearing coaching. Joanne and Bob smothered Ben with kisses as we waited for Gavin to be released. They all made such fools of themselves that I hid behind large sunglasses, embarrassed for them. We finally headed toward my car, the boys skipping ahead playfully. I slowly walked behind them while Jason and his parents followed me, a video camera rolling.

"Such a high-risk pregnancy, yet she can come to a game, Jason Paul," Joanne shrilled.

"How is she even able to walk, sonny boy?" Bob teased.

"I hope it isn't too much on the baby," Joanne added.

I continued along, stupefied. The boys looked back at me—Gavin shocked, Ben disgusted. I looked into their eyes and was overcome with tranquility. Jason and his parents had hit an all-time low, and I was comforted in knowing evil would not prevail. The boys followed my dignified lead. We quietly got in the car, and I gracefully drove away.

"What's wrong with them?" Ben asked once we were in the clear.

"They're nuts, baby. They're nuts." I couldn't help myself.

"Did you see that play I made, Mommy?" Gavin asked. He

carried a heavy burden, always trying to defuse the tension.

"I did! You played a great game!" I exclaimed, but Gavin always sensed my underlying sadness.

I held on to hope that the trial would be delayed, and that in the meantime, someone would come to their senses and dismiss the nonsense from my life.

~

Later that week, my phone rang. I dreaded seeing Barry's number on my cell phone. I'd come to expect the worst news and hated being at the mercy of others who informed me of my fate. I took a deep breath and answered.

"The trial is delayed until after the baby is born," Barry began.

"That's great! I can have a few months of peace," I replied.

"Not so fast," he added. My heart sank. "The referee awarded Jason every weekend with the boys."

I was speechless. A knifing cramp shot through my left side as the baby kicked hard.

"And in addition to his regular dinner visits, he will be responsible for taking them to and from all after-school activities," Barry continued.

The room spun, and my body weakened. All quality time and rights to my children were being ripped from me. I gasped and leaned on the table to steady myself.

"Wait, so I'll basically only see them some evenings to do homework and put them to bed?" I took short, labored breaths.

"Pretty much," Barry agreed somberly.

"For how long this time?" My heart raced. I was shaking.

"Indefinitely. I fear it's an indication of where this ref's headed with custody," he warned.

Every part of me trembled. "What can we do? There has to be something we can do," I pleaded.

Barry submitted a motion to appeal. The purpose of the hearing had been solely to determine if trial should be temporarily adjourned. He made it clear that no decisions regarding custody and visitation were to be made, citing the law guardian wasn't present. He built a strong argument, concluding the order was unduly punitive.

I anxiously waited for his call with news the appeal was granted.

It was denied.

The referee's decision rocked my world. I crumbled into a depression. My boys were slipping away, and I sensed my support system was too. Mom wasn't able to process what was happening. My friends seemed tired of my drama. Theo tried to comfort me, but I was inconsolable. I spent the last couple months of my pregnancy feeling like I was lying on a dungeon floor shackled and hunched over in despair. Time with my boys felt like scraps of bread and water. I saw a grated window high above me, the sunlight clear but out of reach, to be enjoyed by everyone but me. I gasped for air, unable to breathe. I believed I was a decent person, but I began to question what I was being punished for. I wanted to fall to my knees and plead, "I'm sorry. I'm so sorry. Please forgive me, and please let me have my babies back. Please, I'll be good. I'll follow the rules. Please just let me have my children."

chapter nineteen

ON JANUARY 7, 2008 I GAVE BIRTH TO A HEALTHY BABY GIRL. Theo glowed with love and affection. I felt his heart wrap around us as I held Phoebe in my arms. I looked down at her and thought, *please, God, let her always know pure love.* I swore I wouldn't let anything, or anyone, hurt her. I knew childhood wounds could be life altering and persistent.

Later that night, Theo brought the boys to the hospital to meet their little sister. Tears filled my eyes as I witnessed my little boys' love for their sister. My heart warmed with hope as love burned through my pain.

We brought Phoebe home the next day, but the euphoria I rode high on at the hospital dulled as we approached our town. My surroundings reeked of Jason's presence, and I felt the heaviness of his existence weighing on me. That evening as I listlessly unpacked the hospital bag, I discovered a ring box mixed in with the baby supplies. I looked up at Theo. He had a big smile on his face.

"Will you marry me?" he asked tenderly.

"Yes," I replied, but I couldn't raise my energy to match the joy of the moment. The love that surrounded me was overshadowed by my obsession with the custody battle. I was anxiously waiting for the forensics report and for our original visitation schedule to be reinstated.

∽

When my lawyer finally called to tell me the forensics report was ready, he sounded downhearted.

"What does it say?" I asked, both needing to know and dreading the answer.

"I think it's best if we meet in my office," he replied.

I packed the diaper bag, put Phoebe in the infant carrier, and drove to Barry's office. It was near a busy Prospect Isle Mall I used to shop at with my mom. We'd spent hours on my wedding registry and again on the baby registry when I was pregnant with Gavin. It seemed ironic that I'd once frequented the area to set up my life, but now it was where I had to go to deal with it falling apart. I needed my mom desperately, but there was no fight left in her; she seemed to shut out stuff that used to get her riled up. These days, I saw moments of lucidity that revealed a gentler side, like the moment she met Phoebe in the hospital. Tears welled in Mom's eyes as she cradled the baby in her arms. I think she realized she would be leaving her kids and grandkids too soon. I wondered how it felt to be aware you were slipping away. Her face softened, and I could feel her relief in knowing I now had Phoebe to continue the mother-daughter bond.

When I arrived at Barry's office, he smiled at the baby in the infant carrier but wouldn't make eye contact with me. His somber demeanor indicated he had bad news, but I took it to mean he was disgusted with me. I absorbed the energy of others with such intensity that I took responsibility for their moods. He led me to the conference room door and ushered me in. My file was already on the table. I gently placed the infant carrier down and sat with slumped shoulders, one hand holding the edge of Phoebe's carrier, the other clenching my jeans.

Barry sat down across from me, sighed, and opened the re-

port. "It's not good," he began. "I'll start with the recommendation." He flipped to the end and read Levine's words aloud: "I
recommend joint physical custody in which the children will
alternate weeks between each parent's home. I recommend joint
legal custody with the mother responsible for decisions related
to health and religion, and the father responsible for decisions
related to education and extracurricular activities."

I heard a ringing in my ears and felt the color drain from my
face. Overcome with nausea, I covered my mouth to hold back
the bile rising in my throat. I pictured packing the boys' little
bags every other week as they shuffled back and forth between
my house and Jason's. *He'll pick on Ben. They won't have sheets on
their beds. Their clothes will be filthy. He won't help them with homework. He'll influence them with his sick ways.* I trembled as I realized how overbearing Jason's presence would become.

"How can this be?" I asked, my voice barely a whisper. I
shrank in my seat. I felt responsible for dragging my boys, Theo,
and my newborn into my mess.

Barry slowly flipped through the pages, trying to find an answer. "I will say the findings don't match the recommendation."
For the first time, his voice was softer. I hoped that meant there
was a bright side. I needed to be seen in a good light.

"What does it say?" I wanted him to just tell me already. I
was sitting a few feet away from a report about me and my kids,
but I wasn't allowed to touch it. There was a strict court rule that
forensics reports could never get in the hands of the parties, just
the attorneys.

"Well, to start, your ex's test results aren't good." Barry
traced his finger over some lines. "He stirs trouble, then acts like
the victim of the trouble he created. He has anger issues."

Barry shook his head, indicating he concurred.

"What do my tests say?" I asked.

"The mother is polite and respectful of authority," Barry read. "Organized and structured."

"So how does Levine recommend such a drastic change based on that?"

Barry sat up straight with the confidence and strength I'd seen when I first retained him. He continued to read. "The father showed contempt toward the mother during a family session, referring to her as 'she' or 'your mother' in front of the boys, while the mother referred to him as 'Jason' or 'Daddy'."

"What does he say about the kids?" I asked.

"He states here that both boys made it clear they don't want any changes." Barry lifted his shoulders, unable to make sense of Levine's recommendation. "He goes on to say that the law guardian submitted a recommendation asserting there's no need for changes," he added, talking more to himself than me.

"C'mon, Barry. This is bullshit," I said angrily, coming out of my trance. "There has to be a way to fight this." The forensics report was a big win for my ex. Barry knew it would be difficult to fight it in court, and he had too much of an ego to fight a losing battle. I feared that meant he would give up on me.

"Well, it does say here you told Ben your ex was sick in the head," he said dryly.

"Barry, I told you that story already. Does he mention *why* I said that? Does he say what Jason did to Ben that day?" I moaned.

"The report doesn't get into the details, but you did say it. Levine also considered it poor parenting to lie to Gavin about a lost stuffed animal and prevent him from developing skills to deal with a loss," he added.

"I replaced a child's puppet, for God's sake!" I'd had it.

"Well, the doc didn't agree with your approach," Barry retorted. "It also mentions you took Ben to a therapist because you were concerned about him being effeminate?" Barry asked.

"*What?*" I flipped. "I took Ben to see that doctor when he was three or four, because his dad was abusing him! Jason was putting him down, twisting his arms, pulling his hair, spitting on him, and basically going nuts that he couldn't control the kid. I told the doctor that Ben had to sleep in Jason's stepdaughters' room during overnight visits and that Jason treated him like one of the girls. Jason encouraged a macho bond between Gavin and his stepson and forged a duo that excluded Ben. The doctor called Jason in to discuss his treatment of Ben, but Jason became hostile and warned the doctor not to see his son anymore," I explained.

Barry blinked several times like he was trying to follow it all.

"After that doctor wouldn't work with us anymore, I actually tried Levine, without Jason's involvement, but Levine told me he couldn't accept our insurance," I explained.

"Wait, you consulted with Levine privately before the custody battle?" Barry leaned forward, an eager look in his eye.

"Yes," I said, oblivious to why that mattered.

"And he still took the forensics assignment?" Barry said in disbelief.

I nodded. "The referee asked if all parties were fine with that. I only had one consultation with him." I recalled Stuart, my first attorney, assuring me it was fine.

"That's a conflict of interest!" Barry exclaimed.

"I don't know," I said, still focused on the bullshit version of what went down with the first shrink. "I eventually used Dr.

Lauren Walker anyway," I added, explaining how we wound up at a third shrink.

"I see that here." Barry went back to the report. "She states the boys are very well taken care of by you. She notes Ben struggles with his dad, and Gavin is often put in the middle." Barry shook his head, as if the complexities of my family drama was too much to sift through.

"So what the hell's going on that I'm missing why Levine's recommending a change in custody?" Barry stared at me. Perhaps he wanted to hash it out with me, but I was paranoid that he was judging me.

I started to wonder if I was a really bad person who didn't grasp reality. I thought maybe I deserved this. I stared at Barry in shock. His eyes warmed, and he seemed to feel sorry for me. He flipped back through the report and read a few more findings out loud.

"The pediatricians report the boys are thriving under the mother's care. The school reports the boys excel academically and socially and appear to be well taken care of at home." He sounded pleased. "Several witnesses spoke highly of the mother, describing her as loving, devoted, and capable." Barry continued with the praise, but I wondered if I had them all fooled. "The maternal grandparents have been married for forty years." He read the bland statement about my parents. *How unremarkable*, I thought. "The paternal grandparents, divorced since the father was a young boy, were models of amicable co-parenting. Their relationship exemplified the ideal arrangement for children of divorce." Barry's tone turned sour again.

"Are you kidding me? They hate each other!" I couldn't believe what I was hearing. I recalled the day Bob confided in me about Joanne's instability, their volatile relationship, and how often he'd been estranged from Jason. "And my parents get no credit for being married for forty years and raising a family?" What a waste, I thought. "Speaking of credit, do I get any credit for staying in the same neighborhood as this jackass? I bought a house close enough for him to have regular contact with the boys." I wanted the gesture to work in my favor, even though I'd done it out of fear.

"He did mention your homes somewhere in the report." Barry flipped through the pages again. "Here . . . 'The mother's home was clean and well organized. The boys had a comfortable bedroom, clean bathroom, plenty of food, a playroom, and a large fenced backyard. Their school is within walking distance, just down the street. When visiting the father's home unannounced, I came into a mess. Clothes were strewn all over the place, the kitchen counters were covered in clutter, and dirty dishes were piled in the sink. I was told they had just had a family party, and we had to reschedule my visit. On the day I returned, the house was in order.'"

I exploded. "What the hell is that?"

"Look, it's a shitty recommendation that makes no sense, but the court will focus on the summary and not the substance. They'll only care that Levine suggests full custody be taken from the mother to award joint custody to the father."

Barry was scaring me. He was dealing with a client who was losing badly. I knew he had a big ego, and I feared if he couldn't win the case, he would desert me. I didn't realize it at the time, but Barry made me feel the way my father often did. I would be left with the guilt and shame he projected on me when faced with his own shortcomings.

"Come up with a schedule. It doesn't have to be alternating weeks, but it has to be fifty-fifty. There's no way your ex will settle for less with this recommendation in his back pocket." Barry's flat tone told me he'd detached himself. The loss was mine, not his. Unwilling to deal with my cause any longer, Barry dismissed me.

"I'll set up a meeting to try and settle." He offered the bare minimum of service. He didn't have the same care he'd exhibited during our first consultation when he'd promised me the world as he took my money.

"Okay." I was somehow able to sound hopeful, like I could still control the result by drawing up a schedule that Jason would accept. I took a deep breath, acknowledging the parameters I had to deal with, accepting the rules. I was at the mercy of the recommendation, Barry's suspicious judgment, and Jason's inexplicable power. Even faced with losing custody of my kids, I accepted the opinions of others instead of fighting for what I knew was right.

Barry packed up my file and walked out of the conference room. I gathered the diaper bag and carried Phoebe down the hall. Barry's secretary glanced up at me. She'd been working with Barry long enough to recognize my despair. She forced a small smile but quickly looked away so as not to mislead me with encouragement. She made me more nervous than Barry did.

I drove to the mall. That's what Prospect Isle moms did during the day. I was so numb and dizzy I didn't remember driving there. I pushed the stroller in a trance, surrounded by the smell of heavily buttered pretzels and the distant noise of shoppers in the background. I sensed my surroundings, but I was not in my body.

I called my older brother, desperate for his straight-up, quick-fix advice.

"This is such bullshit. Is he paying someone off?" he fumed. "He doesn't even want the kids. You know what you should do?" Dominick asked, and I grew hopeful. "Next time you're in court say, 'Your Honor, I can't afford this. My ex can have custody; I'll take visitation.'" He took a quick pause then delivered the punch line: "Trust me, that asshole will drop them at your front door after two weeks and never bother you again."

"I can't go to court and hand over custody. It's too risky," I said, deflated. He was probably right, but I certainly wasn't going to take that chance.

"So what are you going to do?" he asked, making it clear I didn't seem to have a better plan.

"I don't know. I can't take any more of this." I broke down, sobbing.

"Where's the baby?" Dominick sounded worried.

"She's in her stroller next to me. I don't even remember taking care of her today. I know I changed her and fed her, but it's like I don't even remember doing it," I admitted.

"That's exactly what this asshole is trying to do. He's trying to ruin your life. He's trying to break you." He was almost screaming. "You're so worried about losing the kids, you're losing your life. Stop giving him that power. Fuck him."

I grasped at the only place I thought I had power. "My lawyer told me to come up with a draft schedule. Maybe the attorneys will work something out." I knew I sounded pathetic and weak.

"All right, let me go—I have a meeting," he said, frustrated he couldn't talk any sense into me.

My head hung as he ended the call. Everyone was giving up on me. I desperately wondered who else could help.

~

Later that night, I fed and changed Phoebe. She was such an in-nocent bundle of love in her pink onesie; it killed me that I couldn't even remember my day with her. Jason had me trapped in a fun house that he built and controlled. I hated myself for being too stupid to figure out how to escape while he chuckled at the surveillance monitors watching me try. Now he was taking time with my daughter from me. Theo gushed and fussed over Phoebe with the natural elation and love of a new daddy. I knew how he felt—I felt it too—but my pain dulled my joy. It was like I saw Theo and Phoebe through mirrors, living life in another realm. I was thankful that Theo was so over the moon. I knew the baby was getting all the attention she needed, and I hoped per-haps no one would notice I wasn't there.

Once everyone was asleep, I called my friend Kristine.

"I got the forensics report today. It recommended one week at Jason's and one week at my house, back and forth."

"Are you shitting me?" she roared.

"I can't believe it." I felt as if I'd had the wind knocked out of me.

"What are you gonna do?" She sounded as stunned as I felt.

"I don't know. I have to try and come up with a schedule that's like fifty–fifty but not."

"Who the hell goes back and forth like that? And to a lunatic, no less?"

"I know, Kristine. Meanwhile he's been taking them like practically every day, as you know, and they can't take it anymore. Gavin punched the table the last time that asshole beeped out-side. They're exhausted, they never get to see their friends, and they don't get any homework done over there, so they have to do it all late when they get home." I was drained just telling her about the chaos we'd been living in.

"Can't they just tell him they don't want to go?"

"They do tell him, but according to the judge, it's my responsibility to encourage a relationship with their father. Can you believe this crap? Meanwhile, most times he doesn't even stay with them when he picks them up. He either drops them off at Dottie's sister's or a neighbor's house."

I shuddered. There were nights I didn't know where my own children were sleeping.

"Maybe turn his dinner night into an overnight?" Kristine suggested. "And add a few hours to his alternating weekend?" she added, as if tossing Jason a bone would work.

After a few hours on the phone, at about 1:30 in the morning, I wound up with a color-coded calendar of a fifty–fifty arrangement that I thought I could live with. The question was, would Jason agree?

chapter twenty

THE NEXT MORNING, THEO'S ALARM WENT OFF FOR WORK. I couldn't bear the thought of getting through another day. I grabbed his arm before he was able to get up, and I began to sob.

"What's wrong?" he asked, still groggy.

"I can't take the custody battle anymore," I cried. I'd gone to bed after 2:00 a.m. and hadn't been able to sleep. The color-coded calendar kept flashing in my mind, a blaring reminder of how little time I'd have with my sons.

Theo cradled me in his arms. "I'm so sorry," he said. "I wish I knew how to make it stop. Do you want me to stay home today?"

"Don't worry," I said after a few minutes. "I'll be fine. You need to get ready for work." I felt so bad putting him through all of this, emotionally and financially.

I dragged myself out of bed when I heard Phoebe cry. I was losing the pregnancy weight, and my hair, from stress. My eyes were sunken, with dark circles beneath them. My skin was an ashen gray. Refusing to succumb to depression, I forced myself to be an energetic, engaged mother throughout the day until I could hit the pillow and crash, as if a good night's sleep would refresh my life.

~

That weekend I got Phoebe and myself dressed for church services. I wasn't much of a churchgoer myself, but Theo had asked me to participate in a forty-day blessing for Phoebe, a Greek Orthodox tradition when a baby is born.

I was distraught over the forensics report, exhausted from taking care of an infant and two young boys, and depressed that I was attending a function for my daughter that my boys weren't part of because they were at their father's again. I had no interest in the service but felt I had to oblige. After all, Theo was putting up with so much crap with my ex.

Twenty minutes later, we walked up to the church and found my mother-in-law waiting eagerly on the front steps.

"Hello!" She beamed. "Happy forty days, princess!" she exclaimed in a heavy Greek accent as she grabbed Phoebe from my arms.

I faked a polite smile. Theo's mother didn't approve of me or my divorced status, but she was cordial now that I had given her a granddaughter. I tried to go along with the superficial niceties, but I resented being played for a fool.

I stood in church listening to prayers I couldn't understand, fuming that I was denying myself yet again. After the service, I graciously thanked the priest and said goodbye to my mother-in-law, but inside I burned with rage. I was so sick of everyone taking over my life and my children, but I didn't know how to stand up to Theo and his controlling family. Instead I held in my anger, because I feared what would happen if I let it all out. To make matters worse, I was at a loss for how I'd wound up in a culture more overbearing and unsophisticated than the one I came from. I was disgusted with myself for not being able to live a more cultivated life and ashamed that I couldn't live up to my mother's expectations of me.

~

Later that week, I put on the same outfit I'd worn to church as I got ready for the settlement meeting with Jason and the attorneys. My parents came over to watch Phoebe. My dad had to be with Mom to babysit these days. I hurried around my kitchen laying out bottles and instructions while my father bombarded me with questions about the meeting.

"What did your lawyer say?" he asked.

"I told you already. He said to try and present a schedule that Jason will accept."

"And what if he doesn't accept?" he pressed.

"I don't know. Then I guess it goes to trial." I wished he'd stop asking the questions I was doing my best to avoid.

"What happens if it goes to trial? Will they give him the kids?" His anxiety was worse than mine.

"I don't know!" I snapped. "Just watch the baby."

My mother stood over Phoebe, who was napping in her bassinet, and smiled down at her, not registering what was going on.

I gently kissed Phoebe's head and stormed out the door. I drove to Barry's office with angry thoughts running through my head about everyone in my world: my ex, my parents, the referee, the attorneys, the Greeks, the annoying suburban mothers who acted like they had perfect lives. I hated everyone. I wanted to run away with my kids. I tried to compose myself as I parked the car and walked into Barry's office building. I smiled at people in the elevator as if I were a successful woman going to work.

Barry and the law guardian, Abe, were already in Barry's conference room when I arrived. They both looked up at me with pity, making it obvious they had been discussing my unfortunate case.

"Hello," I meekly said. They nodded, and Barry gestured for me to take a seat.

"The recommendation is not in the best interest of the children," Abe began. "Let's suggest giving Dad some extra time with the boys for a few weekends and some extra dinners to make up for missed visits."

"Most of his missed visits are his own doing," I barked. The second I realized they weren't agreeing with fifty–fifty, I raised my voice like a sidekick hiding behind a bully.

"Just appease him. It's better than trial. Trial could go on for months and cost a fortune," Abe counseled me. "And then you'll be at the mercy of the referee's decision," he added to convince me.

"Fine." I went along with their plan. I felt better knowing I had their sympathy and support, but I was frustrated that they seemed impotent to really help. We made a little strained small talk until Jason and Nick arrived. Barry's secretary showed them into the conference room. Jason's arrogance permeated the air. "Gentleman." He flashed a huge smile at Barry and Abe.

Abe and I exchanged a glance, acknowledging Jason's outward disregard for my presence.

"Good morning." Nick shook our hands. "Thank you for arranging the meeting," he said to Barry.

"Okay, let's get to it," Barry began. "I know Mr. Gladstone here supports me in saying the recommendation of alternating weeks is not in the best interest of the children. It's disruptive and chaotic, especially in a contentious situation." He moved his arms slowly in the direction of me and Jason.

Nick stared blankly. Jason squirmed to the edge of his seat, elbows on the table, pretending to be interested in hearing what Barry had to say.

"We want to offer some extra parenting time to Mr. Axcel," Barry went on, "in part to make up for missed visits and in part to afford him more time with his sons." He tried to sound generous.

"I have a list of suggested days that I would recommend." Abe took over. "I think we can all agree this more than addresses why we got here in the first place." He slid a copy in front of each of us. Nick and Jason glanced over it, but Nick already knew what he had to do.

"We appreciate your attempt to mediate, but at this time my client is not willing to accept a settlement. We plan to proceed with a trial, which"—he looked at his planner as if this wasn't that big of a deal—"I believe is set to commence very soon, in March."

Barry and Abe looked at each other. The meeting was clearly a waste of time. I hung my head and stared at the paper in front of me. I was practically giving away the kitchen sink, but Jason didn't want more time with the boys; he wanted to win and destroy me. He also wanted to stop paying child support. Joint custody meant no more checks to me.

Barry tried to salvage the negotiations. "It's a generous offer of time to your client. The report doesn't paint Mr. Axcel in the best light," he added. "Who knows how the court will interpret the findings?"

Jason and Nick got up from their chairs, signaling the meeting was over.

"Let's see what the ref does with it." Jason patted Nick on the back.

"Thank you for your time," Nick said over his shoulder as they walked out.

"He's impossible," I said to Barry and Abe, who sat dumbfounded. "He'd rather go through a trial and destroy me than agree to a schedule right now."

"Well, he doesn't have to pay his attorney. And he obviously never has to go to work. He can afford to go to trial," Barry said. "But there's something else here. Something's not right."

Abe sighed and packed his briefcase. "I guess I'll see you both in a few weeks. Let's see what we can do then," he added, as if we'd have another shot at reason right before trial began.

~

My anxiety worsened over the next few weeks as I awaited the trial. There was a calm silence from all parties, which unnerved me more than the usual chaos. Jason's smile grew wider and wider each time he came to pick up the boys. He'd stand at the edge of my driveway, giddy with anticipation, eager for his long-awaited day in court with me. My insides churned with a combination of rage, frustration, fear, weakness, and despair. I longed for the joys of motherhood and the bliss of a stable family life, but Jason kept stealing them from me. I was creating a new family with Theo, but it came at a tremendous price: my boys and my peace of mind. I couldn't enjoy anything I had, because I was losing so much.

~

On the eve of trial, the boys happily played about the house while I fed Phoebe on the couch. My own nerves were so frayed, I couldn't think straight. My skin tingled with anticipation. I was far from the image of a beaming mom. I sat in ratty clothes with frizzy hair, my cheekbones protruding beyond my eye sockets. I knew I looked crazed, but I didn't care. I tried to float to another dimension so as not feel my raw reality.

My phone was on the arm of the couch when it rang. I glanced over Phoebe's little head and saw Jason's cell number on the screen. I didn't pick up. I put her in her cradle and then listened to the message. It seemed to be a pocket dial.

"What's next for him? Appointed to judge?" I heard Jason ask.

I couldn't make out what the other person said, but it sounded like his attorney, Nick.

"What's it worth to him?" Jason asked again.

Nick mumbled some response, but it still wasn't clear.

"How far would he go?" Jason asked.

"He would do it," Nick replied. "He'd fix the case."

chapter twenty-one

I REPLAYED THE VOICEMAIL OVER AND OVER AGAIN AS I DROVE to court the next morning. It was almost too good to be true. My anxiety was replaced with a skeptical sense of calm. I had played the message for Theo, my friend Kristine, and my brother Dominick the night before, because I couldn't believe my ears. They all heard it: "Fix the case." Jason and Nick were bribing the referee with a monetary reward, a promise of a seat on the bench, or both.

"Have these pricks arrested! Take it to the DA!" my brother urged. I could taste the vindication. I didn't know how it would work out, but I knew it would. At the very least, I wouldn't show up as a frail, broken victim for a change.

But the part of me that was conditioned by fear remained activated. I couldn't fully relax. I called Barry from the car to fill him in; he hadn't answered the night before.

"It's illegal to wiretap his phone," my attorney advised.

"I didn't wiretap him. *He* pocket dialed me!" I explained. *Why was I always the one under suspicion?* I thought bitterly.

I walked through the metal detector with butterflies in my stomach and met Barry by the stairs. He was easy to spot at over six feet tall with a wide build. He wore a double-breasted designer suit and an expensive watch. I stood tall and slender next to him in high heels and a dress I would have worn to work. "Attractive yet conservative" was how I'd been told to dress for court. We tried to listen to the recording, but we were distracted by the other people around us. A social worker was trying to get a young woman to cooperate with certain procedures.

"I ain't peeing in no cup," the young mother exclaimed as she cradled her toddler on her hip.

Barry and I shared a look. *What am I doing here?* I thought.

I looked down the dimly lit hall and saw Nick and Jason walking in together. Jason was all smiles as he walked with confidence and ease. He swung his arms, eager to get started with the trial. Nick pulled a dolly full of boxes behind him. *What the hell do they have in those boxes? The O. J. glove?* They were so absurd, I almost laughed.

The law guardian, Abe, walked down the hall. He chastised Nick and Jason. "It's ridiculous that we're here today."

"Good morning, Mr. Gladstone." Jason practically chuckled at Abe's lack of power.

We filed into Abruzzi's courtroom, and I realized I wasn't nervous. I knew the truth of who I was as a mother, plus I held the pocket-dial card. Suddenly these men didn't seem so mighty anymore; they kind of seemed like idiots. I was the mother. I knew what was best for my boys. Jason's attention to them was rooted in hate for me. When it came to my kids, I was rooted in love. Love would win.

We stated our names and addresses for the record. The formalities of the court process usually rattled me, but now they seemed dull. I was annoyed at having lost myself in fear of it for so long.

After identifying himself as attorney for the children, Abe began with an opening statement. "There's no need for changes, the children do not want any changes, and the fact that we're in court listening to opening arguments is ridiculous," he firmly said.

Wow, I thought. *That ought to do it.*

"Thank you," Abruzzi said. "Will the attorney for Mr. Axcel please call your first witness to the stand?"

Abe took his seat. My eyes grew wide. We were officially on trial. I didn't think it would ever get this far.

Nick called Jason to the stand and asked him a few rehearsed questions, none of any importance. Jason's voice was subdued as he answered, like it broke his heart that it had come to this. *Give me a break.* I couldn't bear to listen to his bullshit. Barry scribbled notes on his legal pad while I stared into space, pondering my life. *How did I get here? Where did I go wrong?*

We had a couple of brief appearances like this over the next several weeks, but I tuned it all out. I was focused behind the scenes, making calls and sending letters to any agency I could think of to get someone to investigate my case.

I met with a private investigator that my dad's friend recommended. I sat across from him in his basement office, but I could barely see him through his cigarette smoke. I rushed through my story while looking over my shoulder. I'm not sure if I was afraid I'd be shot, or if I was afraid that this was my circle of people. I couldn't wait to get out of there.

Finally, I got through to the Mission County District Attorney's Office and was connected to the Division of Public Corruption. I gave a very brief explanation of my case over the phone, and to my delight, they set up an appointment for me to come in. I felt powerful as I drove to the DA's office on the day of my appointment. It felt good to be in control instead of being the defendant. I awkwardly fumbled with Phoebe's stroller as I was buzzed into the Public Corruptions Unit and was greeted by a middle-aged man dressed in brown. He shook my hand and got right to business. I handed him a tape recording of the message, and he asked me to take a seat in the waiting room. Phoebe, who was just a few months old, had been to more legal meetings than most people attend in a lifetime.

My palms were sweaty as I eagerly waited for the man in brown to reappear. I felt embarrassed sitting there with my baby while strangers looked into my state of affairs. Maybe I was no better than the lady who'd refused to pee in the cup.

Finally, the door opened. "We're ready to see you now," the man in brown said.

I made my way to a tiny interrogation room, where I fumbled with the stroller again. I guessed they didn't typically have to accommodate babies.

"The recording is fuzzy, but we're able to make out some of the exchange between your ex and his attorney. It's enough to open a case," he said.

"Okay, great!" In my mind the DA's office was going to lock Jason, Nick, and the referee up at that moment. But they had a few questions. I forced myself to be patient, like a child waiting for candy.

Most of their questions were related to Jason's role at the town of Rocky Bluff and his association with some prominent names I recognized. I had a naive, self-absorbed perspective that my custody case was the center of the world, so I didn't suspect they could be questioning me about more important matters. The DA handed me an index card with my case number and told me they'd be in touch. Jason, Nick, and company were officially under investigation for corruption. I walked out with perfect posture, relieved that the authorities finally saw me as the good one, the innocent victim.

~

I called my parents from the car.

"What happened?" my father anxiously asked.

"They opened a case," I said. "Put Mommy on." I wanted to talk to her, not him.

"She's right here. Lily, the DA is investigating that son of a bitch," my father shouted.

"What happened now?" she asked, not fully following but conditioned for chaos. As if my saga wasn't enough, my older brother had recently divorced a woman we adored, and my younger brother was living a reckless, Vegas-inspired lifestyle. Cousins and neighborhood friends were gossiping about our family. Their cattiness cast a dark shadow over my mom.

"It's Francesca, for God's sake." My father had no patience for her. "She met with the DA's office this morning." He'd never spoken to her respectfully, but his demeaning tone worsened as he grew more frustrated with her condition.

I regretted calling them. My shoulders slumped as I got sucked into the familiar dynamic between us all.

"How much is this case going to cost?" my father asked. I think he relished in my mess, so he could bail me out and then insult me for needing him.

"There's no cost, Dad," I angrily replied. "Let me talk to Mom."

"Francesca?" my mother said. "Are the kids okay?" She was always worried about us all. I never got to support her; she was always supporting me.

"Yeah, Mom," I softly replied. I knew she had Alzheimer's, but I sometimes wondered if it was wisdom, as if she chose to drift to a new dimension above a darkened world that couldn't rise to meet her brilliance.

~

I spun around my house doing random chores, trying to rid myself of the bad feelings that stirred in me after the call with my parents. I called my brother, hoping to unload their toxicity on him.

"Stop telling them about the case," Dominick advised. "Don't let them know your business." It never occurred to me to detach. It took me a few months to actually try it out, but once I did, it turned out to be the best advice I received.

I eventually called Barry to fill him in on the case at the DA's office. I was hoping it would provide an immediate remedy, but Barry wanted to give some thought to how, and when, we could use it in Family Court. We'd been burned before when attempting to appeal Abruzzi's temporary orders. We'd recently learned the judge who supervised Abruzzi was a former partner at Nick's law firm. Barry wanted to go over their heads. He was considering pleading my case to the administrative judge, the head of the family court. I was frustrated that I'd have to endure yet another custody trial appearance while Barry strategized.

I found myself back in Abruzzi's courtroom, numb to the bone, listening to Jason's endless bullshit. Abruzzi looked at his watch and noted we'd be breaking for lunch soon.

"Your Honor," Nick said, "before we break, can we address the matter of summer visitation? My client is trying to schedule some time and is not getting a response from Mrs. Axcel."

I wished they'd stop calling me that.

Abruzzi shot Barry a questioning look. Barry gave a brief summary of the cute game Jason had played with summer vacation the prior year. Abe chimed in: both parents should have two vacation weeks with the boys. He clarified that a week is seven days, not ten, like Jason seemed to think. I was paying several hundred dollars an hour for grown men to explain to my ex-husband how many days are in a week.

"I suggest you settle this during the break, gentleman," Abruzzi said. (I was always invisible.) "If you can't, I'll issue an order in accordance with the divorce agreement, granting the father two weeks of vacation time," he warned.

Barry stormed out with Abe, but I couldn't help smiling. Abruzzi was so transparent in his bias toward Jason that I was almost embarrassed for him. His orders were practically laughable. A tiny little man in an oversized robe bellowing orders to those who stood several feet below his raised altar, he looked like a cartoon character behind his fake bench.

Nick and Jason whispered like giddy school girls as they caught up with us in the hallway.

"Can we agree to specific weeks for my client?" Nick asked Barry.

"And my client," Barry replied.

"For now, let's focus on vacation time that's already allotted to my client. One day, we can try to modify the divorce agreement to include vacation time for your client," said Nick.

Abe jumped in. "Each parent should be entitled to vacation time."

"Correct me if I'm wrong, but I thought I heard the ref say he would only grant vacation time to the father?" Jason sarcastically asked Nick.

Abe waved his hand in disgust and walked toward the elevator bank.

Barry was purple with anger. Jason's arrogance made people want to punch him in the face.

"I've had it with these corrupt assholes!" I practically screamed. "The DA will take care of them."

Nick swung around and looked toward me, his interest piqued.

"I've had enough of this abuse. Take it to the administrative judge!" I ordered Barry.

Nick cupped his head in his hands and rubbed his temples.

Barry pulled me aside to consult. "Let's be smart about how we proceed here today," he cautioned.

"Barry, I'm done. The criminal case is open. I want a dismissal of this bullshit custody case."

"*Okay*, okay. I'll file a motion with the administrative judge." He finally agreed to fight fire with fire, now that their arrogant bullying had hit his nerve.

"Take your lunch," he barked at Nick. "We won't be negotiating a fixed case."

"I can't have this," Nick whined. "I live my life in a fishbowl." He was referring to his public office and the press coverage that came with it. Did he think we were going to feel sorry for him?

"The ref will take care of it," Jason assured Nick. He didn't think anything could interfere with his plan.

Barry and I grabbed sandwiches and ate together like we'd just pulled off a heist. My appetite, which had been gone for months, suddenly called for a foot-long hero and a bag of chips.

We ran into Abe on the way back upstairs, and Barry quickly filled him in. He raised his eyebrows, and I swear I saw a hint of a smile.

Nick hung his head as we filed back into Abruzzi's room. Barry was ready to pounce, and Abe seemed to be rooting for me. Jason swung his arms, eager to proceed, oblivious to the turn of events.

Abruzzi entered from his back door, believing he still had

power. "Did the parties come to an agreement regarding summer vacation?" he began.

"No." Barry said. "We discussed the criminal investigation before the DA's office."

"Your Honor, if I may"—Nick's voice was shaking—"I'm a public figure. I can't have allegations from the defendant smear my name. I'd like to request a dismissal for the afternoon."

Abruzzi looked stunned. "Counsel?" He looked at Barry and Abe.

"We have no objections to a dismissal," Barry replied.

"We shouldn't be here in the first place," Abe added.

"All right then, we'll break for the day. Let's get back on the calendar. . . ." He looked down at his desk.

"Your Honor," Barry interrupted, "I'm not sure a return date will be necessary." He waited a beat, then added, "I'll be submitting a motion to Administrative Judge Bansky for a recusal and change of venue."

Abruzzi's eyes grew wide. "Very well. Parties are dismissed until further notice from the court."

Barry and I regrouped in the parking lot. I would continue to work with the DA and any other agency who would listen. Barry would prepare the motion to recuse Abruzzi and request a change of venue to another county, where Jason had no political ties. I was relieved Barry was doing his part but even more thrilled at feeling like I could take care of myself.

I called Theo from the car and filled him in. He was at work and had a mild-mannered disposition, so he didn't exude the energy I needed. I called Kristine. She was more of a firecracker, like me. We hooted and hollered, and I drove home the rest of the way with the radio cranked.

Barry eventually called me into his office to sign the motion he prepared. I sat at his conference room table and let out a huge sigh of relief as I read through it. He'd captured every point I'd been trying to make. It felt so good to be acknowledged.

"Thank you," I said as I signed away, giving him credit for finally proceeding the way I'd wanted to all along.

"I'll submit it this afternoon," he said with pride in his work. "Your ex will submit a reply. Let's hope Bansky does right by us."

chapter twenty-two

I SPENT THE NEXT COUPLE OF WEEKS IN ANTICIPATION. I LIVED a lot of my life like that—going through the motions, waiting for some future event. It was always what was next, never now. I couldn't smell the roses, or taste my food, or really absorb all the good in my life. I only saw what was wrong; I didn't know how to be happy. Problems were my pulse, and having them meant I was alive.

A large manila envelope with a family court stamp on the return label finally arrived in the mail. I tore it open and scanned through the administrative judge's decision. I held the papers to my chest and looked up toward the ceiling. Abruzzi was tossed from the case, along with all his bullshit orders. The case was reassigned to Judge Wendy Hoffman. She was still in our county, in the same courthouse. I'd been hoping for Manhattan or Queens Court, but at least Abruzzi was out.

I called Barry.

"I was just about to call you," he answered excitedly. "Big win!" He exclaimed.

"I could kiss you!" I said as I giggled.

"I'm not thrilled that he kept it in the same jurisdiction, though." Barry's tone turned thoughtful. "They're all in bed together. But changing the venue would've been an acknowledgement of corruption in your courthouse. Tough for the administrative judge to do that."

"But everything goes back to how it was?" I asked, desperate to stay focused on good news.

"Yes, after all that, you're back to your original agreement," he confirmed. "But we still need to deal with this case. No drama with your ex in the meantime . . . let this all simmer down. Hopefully, the new judge will dismiss it when we have our first appearance before her . . . looks like in the fall." I was basically being told to be a good girl for the next few months. I was practically in tears. But the feeling of joy was so foreign to me that it made me nervous. I calmed myself down, because I didn't want to jinx it.

I laid low, as Barry had instructed. Jason took it as permission to walk all over me. He abused summer vacation language once again, continued to bombard me with self-serving documentation, and spun everything into litigation and grounds against me. I tolerated it all, because I was so afraid to take one step out of line. Every move I made, every thought I had, was centered on court.

The more I obsessed over the custody battle, Jason, and court, the more they showed up in my life. My heart sank when Barry called a few weeks later. "We need to be in court this afternoon for an emergency order," he said.

I panicked. "What happened now?"

"I have no idea. I'll see you there."

I drove to the courthouse a nervous wreck, fearful there'd been a mistake in Abruzzi's dismissal.

As I went through the metal detectors, my mind raced ahead to what awaited me inside. People were coming and going, and I didn't know which way to look, which way to go. Barry showed up just as jumpy, as if we were both meeting in a hospital emergency room after receiving a dreadful call.

Abe broke the news to us. "Mr. Axcel is getting married on Sunday, August 16, which is technically your weekend. He wants the court to grant him the weekend for his wedding." He rolled his eyes.

"What?" I couldn't believe we'd gotten dragged in for this. Barry threw his arms in the air, pissed that he'd taken time from his busy practice for this nonsense.

I refused. "No way! Theo and I are getting married on Saturday the fifteenth. We chose the date knowing it was *my* weekend."

Barry was incredulous. "You two are getting remarried a day apart?"

"I guess so," I said, annoyed that nothing could be free from Jason.

We wound up agreeing to give Jason the Sunday for his wedding in exchange for an extra weekend for me. The afternoon in court was an unnecessary circus, and it troubled me how easily Jason got the court's attention.

~

I was so lost in the case that I didn't bother to plan a wedding. I didn't even buy an outfit. The morning of the big day, I threw on something from my closet and tried to tame my frizzy hair. Theo and I drove to the justice of the peace with the kids.

"Why aren't you in a dress?" Ben asked.

"Theo really likes this top," I replied, trying to make an excuse for my lack of preparation.

"Why isn't anyone else coming? Why isn't there a party?" Gavin asked.

"We're celebrating as a family. Just us today," I replied.

"We're going out for a nice brunch after the ceremony and then to a fancy restaurant tonight." I tried to talk it up.

We waited in a basement room decorated with the American flag and some local government flags. My stomach turned—the setting reminded me of court. The boys were playful, silly almost. Phoebe slept the entire time in her carrier. Theo and I locked eyes during our vows, and I was jolted into what felt like a parallel universe. I wasn't in the right headspace to get married, but I figured I'd eventually sort it out.

The next day, the boys attended their father's wedding. It took place on the front lawn of his trailer-like home. When they returned, we sat at the kitchen counter eating leftover wedding cake from the day before.

Ben gave his review. "It was a luau theme, but Dottie wore an army dress."

"Supervisor Caputo was the priest," Gavin said. Caputo had held the supervisor post, which was similar to a mayor, for years. Gavin sounded suspicious of why his dad's boss officiated.

"I don't even think Dottie likes Dad," Ben said. "He's mean to her, and she tries to leave."

"But Dad says she would lose her town job, and her kids would have nothing, without him," Gavin added.

Theo retreated to his recliner to watch TV. He seemed annoyed that Jason and the case consumed our life. We didn't go on a honeymoon. I was so paranoid about losing my kids that I had developed irrational fears about leaving them. For years, I came up with excuses to stay tethered to them. I had to prepare for my first appearance before the new judge at the time; there was no way I could go on vacation.

The more I sensed Theo's dissatisfaction with me, the more I scurried about trying to keep him happy. I exhausted myself making sure the house was run the way he wanted it. I sold furniture I loved to make room for the stuff he chose. The air conditioner was set to the temperature he liked, and I stopped drinking bottled water because he preferred tap. I cringed if the boys didn't finish their food—Theo didn't like waste.

He grew up conditioned to believe there was never enough money, and his fear of lack haunted him. To ease his tension, I switched banks to the one he used and relinquished total control of the finances. After all, he was the main breadwinner, and my court battle was a financial drain. I felt I had to ask his permission for everything and wound up shackled in frustration if he deemed my desires unnecessary.

I don't think Theo knew how repressed I felt. He was just living the way he was raised, recreating his parents' marriage. Eventually, a wild animal roared from within me and howled out its savage frustrations. I think I was letting out generations' worth of outrage. I wanted so much to burn Theo's family's *Moron Manual*, it helped me burn mine. It felt so good that once I started screaming, I couldn't stop. I yelled for years. Phoebe became the little girl hiding under her sheets, the way I had when my parents argued. The generational baton is sneaky that way.

chapter twenty-three

"CAN THIS BE REAL?" I ASKED BARRY. THERE WAS A CLERICAL error regarding our court date. The judge's calendar had us slotted for an earlier date than was communicated to us, and we were all no-shows on what should have been our first appearance. I received a letter in the mail that the case had been dismissed.

"It's real!" He chuckled. "Dismissed." He'd received the same notice.

"We're done?" I couldn't believe it.

"Seems that way. I'll close your file and send you a final invoice." It was always about the fees.

Jason wasn't going to let me off the hook that easily. He refiled his petition for custody, and we were ordered to appear in court in December 2008, a few days after we received the order. Barry planned to make an oral argument, supported by Abe, and we all hoped the matter would be dismissed.

I called a friend to watch Phoebe so I could go to court. I had already told my parents the case had been dismissed, and there was no way I was revisiting it with them. Dominick was right—I stabilized a bit as I distanced myself from their spinning.

Judge Hoffman's waiting area was packed to capacity. My nerves electrified as I absorbed the negative energy of everyone there. A court officer opened the door, and I peeked inside. Hoffman's courtroom was much larger and more formal than Abruzzi's. Names were called every few minutes, and each time, I jumped. She was clearly in a rush to move through her caseload.

My palms were sweaty and my heart was pounding by the time we were called.

"Counsel, the matter before the court of *Axcel v. Panagos* will commence trial July 2009," the judge announced.

That's seven months away, I thought.

"Your Honor, if I may?" Barry began. "We are here on an order to show cause based on a petition from the plaintiff. We are entitled to reply. There's no merit to this case. The law guardian for the children supports our position." He nodded at Abe.

"Your Honor, I've said it before, and I'll say it again: there's no basis for a change in custody," Abe chimed in.

"I'm not conducting a hearing on merit. This case was already sent to trial by Referee Abruzzi. Any other matters?" She held her gavel, ready to dismiss us.

"Yes, Your Honor," Barry started again. "The matter of holiday visitation needs to be addressed."

Nick interrupted. "Your Honor, the parties already have a holiday schedule in their divorce agreement."

The judge looked at Barry.

Barry tried to explain. "That's correct, but Mr. Axcel doesn't follow the agreement."

"He follows it," Nick interrupted again. "He is scheduled to be with the children Christmas Eve and the school break this year. Mrs. Axcel has the children for Christmas Day."

"Your Honor, while the majority of that is true, the agreement reads the father has the boys until 10:00 p.m. on Christmas Eve, yet he never returns them at that time," Barry explained.

"Work it out, Counsel. Follow the agreement," Hoffman ordered with a stern frown.

"That's what my client plans to do, Your Honor," Nick said smugly.

"If that's all, I will see all parties in July of 2009." Hoffman dismissed us.

Abe shook his head and walked out.

"She didn't even give us a chance." Barry sounded more rattled than pissed.

"Why did she push the trial out to July 2009?" I asked. The holiday matter was such a lost cause, I didn't even get upset.

"Probably because she knows it's bullshit and hopes it goes away by then. That, or to keep you under the watchful eye of the court," Barry said.

~

Less than a week later, I filed a police report about Christmas Eve as if it were as routine as grocery shopping and laundry. Barry used it to file a visitation violation petition that was returnable before Judge Hoffman. Jason showed up without Nick, and the petition was swiftly adjourned until trial. I stormed out, fuming that Jason seemed to get away with everything.

He owed me thousands of dollars for out-of-pocket medical expenses, extracurricular activities, and camps, but he ignored my attempts to collect. Yet, he seemed to have endless resources to take Gavin all over the country to major sporting events and Ben to an endless run of Broadway shows. (Years later, I learned that town employees had questionable perks).

In retaliation for him suing me for custody, I sued him for the money he owed me. Jason showed up with another low-level attorney from the town to represent him. I had an Excel summary of expenses and receipts. But collecting out-of-pocket expenses was not as straightforward as child support. Jason negated most costs, alleging he wasn't aware of said activities and should not be held responsible. He had his own list of expenses in an effort to offset mine. He even tried to convince the judge that he incurred excessive hockey costs, even though neither of my boys played hockey.

I was awarded a very small fraction of what I sued him for. My time and appearances in court weren't worth it. I never asked him for a dime again.

In a final flip of the finger, he began giving Gavin the monthly child support checks.

"Here, Mom. Here's the money Dad gives you," Gavin would say as he handed me a check at the beginning of the month. "Daddy says he pays for everything." Jason was trying to convince Gavin the way he tried to convince other parents when he would hand me checks at soccer games or lacrosse games.

~

With a break from court appearances for a while, Theo and I hosted a neighborhood cocktail party at our house. I was standing in my living room with a drink in my hand, trying to jump-start a new life, when one of the husbands of a nursery school mom approached me.

"Daniela filled me in on the lawsuit with your ex," he said. "I run my business out of the town, so I know who he is," he explained.

"Yeah, it's quite a saga." I wasn't in the mood to discuss Jason.

"Look, I feel a moral obligation to tell you something," he gravely said. "Your ex does less-than-ethical work for Supervisor Caputo and other more powerful government officials. His buddy

Nick is representing him as a favor to some higher-ups. These guys are navigating your ex through the system, and from what I heard, the fix is in."

"I already have a case before the DA." I wanted him to know I wasn't totally clueless, even though I was reeling from his news. "Would you be willing to make a statement?"

"I'm sorry. I'm not getting involved." He raised his hands. "I can't risk my business with the political machine at play in this town." He made it clear he'd offered all the help he could, before adding, "Oh, and don't think the DA isn't in bed. You're making a case in the very arena they all play in. I'd take it to the press or another agency outside of their jurisdiction."

The entire neighborhood was drunk in my house that night. Everyone had a blast—everyone but me. My head was spinning about what Daniela's husband had told me.

Monday couldn't come fast enough. I made some calls to the local newspaper, and a reporter took an interest in the story. We corresponded for a few weeks until I learned she'd suddenly left the paper. Everything smelled suspicious.

The DA was taking too long for my liking. Every time I checked in with them, they told me these things take time. Occasionally, they would call me with questions that I felt were off topic. They asked me for dates of all my court appearances, to determine how often Jason wasn't at his government job. They asked me questions about his boss and a few other political guys, all of whom I knew but were not part of my case. Frustrated by the slow momentum, I decided to cast a wider net.

I'd heard a guy my friend once dated was now an FBI agent. She got me his number, and thankfully he took my call. I filled him in, and he put me in touch with an agent who covered my territory.

"They're worse than the mob, and Nick Napolitano is the worst of the worst," the agent said after listening to my story. He seemed quite familiar with Jason's lawyer and the rest of his cronies.

The FBI opened an investigation. I found the line of questioning and their process to be very similar to the DA's office. Same names, same questions, sniffing around for the same material. No one ever asked about my kids or my custody case. I was frustrated that there were a few open investigations, but none seemed to be helping my cause.

It had been seven years since I changed the locks, but I still wasn't satisfied that Jason got what he deserved. I didn't know how to move on without fully wringing him out. The harder I tried, the more he found clever ways to get to me.

He even ruined the boys' activities for me. Ben auditioned for a local theater and was cast in a production of *The Wizard of Oz*. It launched his love of theater and gave Jason a new stage of his own. Jason attended every performance, whistling and screaming from the audience each time Ben took the stage, hooting wildly when Ben took his bows. People thought he was a supportive father, but I knew he was putting on his own show. Dottie and her kids were always in tow. I wondered why they didn't seem to have activities of their own. Between his boisterous cheering and his entourage, it felt like he was trying to make me smaller by making himself larger.

~

That year, Mother's Day was Jason's weekend, and Gavin had an early lacrosse game. I thought it was rude to have games on Mother's Day, but I was glad for the 8:00 a.m. start. At least I wouldn't have to wait for Jason to drive the boys home, late as always. I would be able to leave the field with them and enjoy the day.

Jason had other plans.

After the game, I waited for the boys on the sidelines.

"Say goodbye to your mother," Jason ordered. "You'll see her again later."

"It's Mother's Day! The boys are with me today!" I couldn't believe it.

"Daddy, it's Mother's Day," Gavin said anxiously.

"Get in the car, boys." Jason's nostrils flared. The boys looked at me with guilt and fear. "Get in the car!" Jason screamed. "You'll see your mother after you have breakfast with Nana and Dottie." They tried to walk toward me, but he grabbed them each by the arm and shoved them into his Jeep.

I sat in my car trembling as I called Abe and left a voicemail at his office. As law guardian for the children, I felt he needed to know about this immediately. I was startled by a knock on my window. Another mom had witnessed the exchange. She eventually submitted a letter to the court on my behalf. The boys finally arrived home late morning, wide-eyed and anxious. I kept my anger in check, but my insides burned.

~

Before I could recover from Mother's Day, Jason emailed me his summer vacation request. I held my head in my hands as I checked my calendar.

"Jason, the weeks you chose are fine. But just to be clear, seven days goes from your Friday to the following Friday. They need to be home for my weekends." I hit send, cringing.

His needling reply was no surprise: "I'm entitled to two weeks. I will begin my weeks at the end of my weekends. Sunday night to the following Sunday. It's silly of you to keep bringing this up. It's clear how the court will interpret it."

~

I'd learned by then not to engage in email wars with him. Instead, I called Barry. I'd have to pay for his time to manage this, again. Barry and Abe tried to set up a conference call to mediate the matter, but Nick never returned their calls.

With Phoebe in her stroller, I picked up the boys from school. They skipped alongside us, and she smiled through her pacifier, clapping. They played peekaboo while we walked, and she giggled. As I approached my house, I saw a gray Chevy parked outside. My heart sank, and my legs went weak. Sure enough, the door flung open, and a thug jumped out with a manila envelope in his hand. He shoved the envelope at my chest and got back in his car.

"Who was that, Mommy?" Gavin asked.

"Court again," I replied.

"Why?" Ben asked.

"Because Daddy wants to ruin my life." I felt no obligation to hide the truth anymore. We walked into the house in silence. I took Phoebe out of the stroller and put her in her high chair. I put snacks and juice on the table for the boys. This was not the fun after-school moment I'd hoped for. Instead of sitting with my kids, I called Barry. Turns out there was an emergency hearing scheduled to grant Jason summer visitation time. Barry wasn't available the day we were ordered to appear; he had a trial then.

Good, I thought. My brother had Broadway tickets for Ben that day, and we were planning to meet in the city for lunch before the matinee. Barry sighed and said he'd deal with it.

He prepared an affidavit highlighting that there was no need for a hearing, because I'd already agreed to Jason's summer vacation weeks. He included the email exchange between Jason and me, and a letter from Abe supporting our position: a week is seven days, and both parents should have two weeks of vacation. Barry made sure to note that he had a trial in another county on the day of the hearing, and Abe noted that he couldn't appear that day either. Barry told me the affidavit had been submitted to the court, and an appearance wasn't necessary.

～

The day of the matinee, I drove to the city with the kids. My cell phone rang with what I recognized as a Mission County number. *Maybe it's the DA with some progress*, I thought as I answered.

"Is this Francesca Panagos?" a woman sternly asked.

My voice trembled. "Yes?"

"This is Judge Hoffman's office. You were due before the court today. You need to appear, or a warrant will be issued for your arrest."

"My attorney submitted a reply in writing," I explained. "He and the law guardian couldn't be there today. He told me I didn't have to appear." I told her exactly what Barry had said to me, but still I felt as if I'd done something wrong.

"The appearance is still on the calendar. Mr. Axcel and his attorney are here to proceed." She didn't soften.

"I'm in New York City. I'm nowhere near court, and my attorney is on trial in another county." I was hyperventilating as a million dark thoughts raced through my mind.

"I suggest you call him," she said tersely, then hung up.

I left Barry a frantic voicemail and sat through lunch in a full-blown panic. Instead of enjoying the day, I twitched with anxiety. My brother could not believe this was how I lived. While he took Ben to the play, I went with Gavin and Phoebe to ESPN Zone. I figured Gavin would get a kick out of it. It was supposed to be my time with him while Phoebe napped in her stroller. We played air hockey and basketball, but I kept checking my phone, waiting for Barry to call.

I was parked outside the theater before it let out. My brother knew I had to rush home because it was a dinner night for Jason.

I sat in bumper-to-bumper traffic on the Prospect Isle Expressway and realized I wouldn't be home in time for Jason's 5:00 p.m. pickup. I called him and explained traffic was bad and we'd probably be half an hour late.

"No problem," he said, which left me wary.

Finally, Barry rang.

"Hello?" I nervously answered.

He started in without any small talk. "Today was not good." I winced at the reprimand I heard in his tone. "I received a call that a warrant was going to be issued for my arrest for failing to appear in your case. I ran over to the courthouse from my trial and was fined $2,500 for Nick's wasted time." I froze while he went on, not daring to interrupt. "The judge will issue a decision on summer visitation, but I can assure you it will not be in your favor," he warned.

"Barry, you told me we didn't have to appear! You told me you and Abe took care of it." I tried to remind him that I wasn't the problem.

"Look, I'm not comfortable being part of whatever is at play here. What more do you know about your ex's role in the town?" He had recently referred to Jason as the "bag man," a low-level thug who paid visits to local businesses and construction sites to collect cash in return for government contracts and permits. But now it seemed Barry suspected far worse.

"I don't know." I was drained. I didn't care about Jason's shady role in the town at that moment. Barry's fine would be added to my bill. And I would have a crappy summer again, with basically one weekend a month for my family to be together.

"This is not good." Barry snapped me out of my fog. "I'll be in touch when the judge issues her order. This will not play out well at trial in July." He hung up.

I finally approached my house and saw a police car and Jason's Jeep at my curb. I parked in my driveway, and the cops emerged from their car.

"Miss, your husband called because you didn't make the boys available for visitation."

"Ex-husband. I called on my way home to tell him I was stuck in traffic." I was done. "For God's sake, I'm thirty minutes late."

"We need to respond to the call and file the complaint." The cops knew this was nonsense.

The boys nervously watched me unload Phoebe from the car, unsure what to do.

"Go to dinner with your father," I said. "I'll see you in a little bit."

"It's okay," I urged when they looked doubtful. I signed the stupid report and went inside.

chapter twenty-four

WE WAITED A FEW WEEKS FOR THE SUMMER ORDER BUT HEARD nothing. Finally, Barry received a copy mailed to him from Nick's office. The judge gave Jason whatever he wanted for summer and nothing for me. No surprise there. But what was surprising was that she moved the trial again, from July 2009 to January 2010. I wondered why Nick's office had a copy but Barry's didn't. Something was off.

Every time I was served with a new order, I played the recording of the pocket dial for a new agency. I had to go tit for tat; it was how I thought I had power. Under the advice of a friend, I went to the Commission on Judicial Conduct, trying to get Jason, Nick, Abruzzi, and any of their cronies disbarred. I drove into downtown Manhattan and sat in a tremendous conference room before a table of older men, probably retired. I felt like a little girl on Santa's lap. They listened sympathetically and told me they would review my case, but by then I wasn't hopeful any of this would come to fruition. I left feeling more frustrated than before. I desperately needed Jason to pay for his behavior. I needed to air my grievances and make it clear that I was worth more than I had tolerated for myself. I'd be damned if I had to move on without restitution. I'd lost too many pieces of myself, and I wanted them all back so I could start over whole, perfect.

Theo was also determined to make Jason pay. He was so frustrated that he took matters into his own hands. The next time Jason and Bob stood on my front lawn waiting for the boys, Theo turned the sprinkler system on. It was funny to watch Jason and Bob jump around getting soaked before scurrying back into their car. But I saw Jason smirk through the windshield. He enjoyed knowing he was getting to us.

"Don't give him the satisfaction," I advised Theo, using my mother's words. "The more he knows he's getting to you, the more he'll torture you." I should've taken my own advice.

Frustrated with Jason's daily presence and his deep connections in our town, Theo and I talked about moving. He eagerly started looking for houses fifty miles away, the maximum distance I was allowed to move. I can't say I blamed him. I fantasized about a clean slate, a fresh start. But I didn't trust it would make a difference. Deep down, I knew my problems would follow me.

Theo wasn't the only one growing tired of my story. I noticed my good friends tried to change the conversation any time it came up. Contessa, my college friend who helped me process this saga over the years, began to challenge my perceived lack of power and questioned if I could try a different way. I was getting the hint that at some point I'd need to move out of victim mode and get my shit together. But I wasn't ready. I was too angry. And I was afraid to let my guard down.

I searched like a scavenger for conversations with people just like me, who would keep the drama alive. Misery loves company, and people who I thought were friends were focused on my drama so they didn't have to look at their own.

I even used therapy as a place to keep telling my story. I'd been seeing Angela, a local social worker, since Jason and I separated. During the custody battle, I used our weekly sessions as an opportunity to rant and summarize the latest details of the court saga. I looked forward to our meetings the way an alcoholic looks forward to a drink.

I claimed I wanted all the drama to be over, but with every email Jason sent, after every provoking antic or late drop-off, I called Barry to complain. He rarely took my calls by then. I was appalled at his lack of focus on my case, so I added attorneys to my growing list of complaints. But deep down, I was annoyed at myself for being the kind of person that stable people tried to avoid.

I was busy with Phoebe when Barry finally called me back, but I'd been waiting for the chance to unload my grievances. "Barry?" I fumbled with my cell phone.

"Yes, hi," he began. "I got your messages. I've been tied up with a new case." He tried to justify his lack of attention to mine. "Look, the more I think about the latest day in court, the more I think I can't really be of service to you. The judge is already pissed at me and favoring Nick. I'm just not sure I can win this for you." He sounded like a college boy trying to gently dump a girl he had no interest in.

I tried to hold on to him. "Maybe they'll wind up arrested or disbarred before the January trial."

"I'm not sure it's wise for me to be taking anyone down." He seemed uncomfortable about whistleblowing. After all, I wasn't his only case before the court. He buttered his bread there and probably didn't want to ostracize himself.

Even if Barry wanted to distance himself from me and any scandal at play, technically an attorney couldn't just drop a client. I had to fire him. He left me with no choice. For once, I realized it was better to be alone than in a bad relationship.

I went to Barry's office for what would be the last time. I had to sign some paperwork and pay my balance so he could release my file to whomever I hired next. I was so ashamed with how my life had turned out, it felt like I was signing proof that Barry wanted no part of me. But as I released him from the tainted woman I was convinced he saw, I felt a little release from her myself. Barry didn't make me nervous anymore. He wouldn't be in my business, judging me, telling me how to proceed. He couldn't scold me or deliver drop-to-my-knees news anymore. He was suddenly just a person with no power over my life.

"Look, you'll get through this," he said softly, as if I were too weak to move on. "Even the worst cases eventually settle down. Your ex will lose interest in the kids in a few years. Or they'll lose interest in him," he said, as if it was the best I could hope for in life. Something inside me knew I deserved better.

"Well, thanks for all you've done. Wish me luck from here," I said as I got up from the table. I rushed out the door, relieved to be on my own. I realized I'd felt more accountable to Barry than to myself while he represented me. Yet, in an instant, he disappeared. I had a strange feeling I could make the case disappear too. But that seemed like magic that only a fool would trust.

chapter twenty-five

I DIDN'T TELL ANYONE THAT I LET MY ATTORNEY GO, BECAUSE I didn't want to be under the influence of their opinions. I didn't want advice. I needed a break from the noise. A sense of calm came over me.

The next morning, I talked to myself while I made a pot of coffee. *Just show up to trial without an attorney. Maybe they'll go easier on you if you're unarmed,* a voice in my head said. *Act like it's no big deal, and then maybe it will be no big deal.* I reached for the coffee pot. *Downplay the severity. Maybe it will be handled like a minor event.* I filled the pot with water.

What kind of an idiot shows up to a custody trial without an attorney? a different voice in my head said. *A reckless mother!* it scolded. *You're asking for trouble. Do you like trouble?* I put the coffee grinds in the pot.

Maybe you would speak with more sincerity than an attorney would. Maybe the judge would connect with you and have a heart, the first voice rationalized. *Maybe everyone will soften and come to an understanding.* I poured coffee in my mug and added milk and sugar. *Like Jason would ever connect and soften,* the latter voice scoffed. *He won't back down. And why should you back down after what that bastard put you through?* My shoulders stiffened. *Don't show up weak. Screw him. Fight the fight!*

I stared out the sliding glass doors toward the yard, lost in thought as I savored my morning coffee. My nostrils flared when

I spotted the neighbor across the way whose son had ridiculed Gavin about his parents being divorced. I looked away, annoyed, and noticed a realtor's business card on the kitchen counter. Theo was ready to list the house.

Another voice in my head spoke: *You really should get away from Jason and his torture. You don't even like Prospect Isle. Plus you're sick of all the nosy neighbors who know your story.* My body straightened in unity with the angry mob in my mind, determined to move out and move on.

But what about the kids? They like it here. They have friends. Too many voices were coming at me at once. *What will happen when Jason picks them up? They'll be so far from home every other weekend. That bastard won't cooperate with their new activities in their new town. They'll miss games, rehearsals, and birthday parties.* I slumped over the kitchen counter. Another voice delivered the final blow. *And do you really want to be bothered settling into another suburb?*

I didn't know which voice in my head to listen to, so I called a psychic I'd been to a few times and set up a phone reading. I needed her to tell me what was going to happen, because I wasn't ready to be held accountable for whatever did. I thought I got clarity during our call, but the relief didn't last long after I hung up. Everything she said could be interpreted according to whatever voice in my head I listened to. I was annoyed at myself for wasting time and money.

But I was really annoyed by a luminescent image I kept seeing in the distance of my mind. I felt drawn to it as it beckoned me to come closer. I snapped myself out of my daydream and disregarded the sensation. I had issues to deal with. The ball of light slowly faded into the distance of my mind, its presence dimly glowing.

I pulled myself together and got back to business. I certainly couldn't risk custody of my children and the stability of my family by listening to psychics or voices in my head. I couldn't waste precious time chasing images that danced in my mind. I had to handle matters prudently. Otherwise I'd be blamed, judged, and criticized for being a fool. Anyone in their right mind would hire another powerhouse attorney, fight the fight in court, and list the house and move.

I made a few calls, and my friend's husband got me a free consultation with a female partner at one of the most prominent law firms in the area. I told Theo to go ahead and call the real estate agent. *Let him handle the transaction,* I thought. I couldn't deal. My one requirement was no sign on the front lawn, I didn't want Jason to catch wind of it.

~

I checked in at the reception desk of yet another law firm, uncomfortably aware of my jeans. I was underdressed, the inappropriate one. I had somehow fallen from grace and was unable to live the big life I once thought I was capable of. My shoulders curled in as I shrunk into the couch where I'd been asked to wait. I wiped my sweaty palms on my jeans and promised myself that if this attorney could fix the mess I was in, I would fix my life once and for all.

A well-dressed, friendly assistant popped into the reception area and called my name. She smiled without judgment, led me down the hall, and offered me bottled water. It felt good to be seen as a person, not just a train wreck.

The female partner greeted me with the same respect. She

looked me in the eyes and smiled as she shook my hand from behind her grand desk and then gestured for me to take a seat. Behind her and to her right were walls of windows, to her left a wall of shelves filled with books and photos. A coffee table and couch area sat between her back and the rear window. If not for some very dumb choices, I could be this powerful woman. She was what people expected of me, what I expected of myself. I was a total disappointment, but I was determined to make a comeback.

"Tell me what's going on," she said with compassion.

I spoke nonstop for forty-five minutes. At one point, I could tell she'd heard all she needed to hear. I could see the wheels in her head spinning a strategy. But she didn't interrupt me, and she didn't cut me off—she let me finish.

When I was finally done, I looked up at her the way I had looked up from the dining room table as a child. I needed her to see the depths of me and reassure me that I would be okay.

"Miss, you're a victim of a screwed-up system," she said. "There's nothing the combined experience of the partners at this firm can do for you. This case is beyond the law."

Time stopped, and all my hope plummeted.

"But here's someone who can help." She scribbled a name and phone number on a yellow sticky note before handing it to me.

I looked up, confused. "Who's Bruce?" I asked.

"He's partners with Judge Hoffman's ex-husband. He represented her ex-husband during their divorce. Judge Hoffman is not allowed to hear any cases that Bruce is on. She won't be able to proceed with your trial. At the very least, your case will have to start over before a new judge." She must have sensed my hesitation about what good it would do to have to start over, because she added, "Sometimes cases that drag on too long become stale and go away."

I looked back down at the yellow sticky note. *Removal of the judge, no trial—a reset button. I'll take it,* I thought.

"Thank you. I'll call Bruce." I put the yellow sticky note in my bag and hugged it tightly under my arm. "I really appreciate your time," I humbly added, almost in tears. A total stranger had shown up in my life and placed a gentle hand on my shoulders.

"I'm sorry you're going through this. I hope it all works out," she said with sincerity. "Oh, and did you ever think maybe you have a book on your hands? It's quite a story."

I laughed. "Yeah—one day." In my mind, I saw the flicker of that light I was trying to ignore.

I drove home in silence—no radio, no calls. I needed to process what had just transpired. I knew the yellow sticky note was special, but it was up to me to activate its power. The sensation went beyond the court case. I had to be ready to move on if I called Bruce.

~

Bruce's secretary answered my call. "Mr. Gentile's office." Bruce was expecting to hear from me. We set up an appointment to meet at his office.

I arrived with Phoebe in her stroller, and we were put in a conference room to wait for Bruce. Phoebe fussed, so I put *Sesame Street* characters on her tray to amuse her. Bruce walked in, a bit taken aback by the baby. His subtle jolt held the mirror up to how out of sorts my life seemed. He quickly recovered and waved hello to Phoebe with the warmth of a nursery school teacher. I stood up slightly from my chair to shake his hand and realized if I stood straight I'd tower over him. But his handshake was strong and confident. He didn't need to compensate for his height—he knew his worth. I liked him immediately.

"I got a little background from the referring attorney, but why don't you tell me the details?" He wasted no time. He listened attentively and scribbled notes on a legal pad while I spoke. He circled key names such as Nick Napolitano, Supervisor Caputo, and Referee Abruzzi. He made a note of Jason's role in the town government and double underlined DA and FBI. I tried to speak calmly while my eyes nervously watched for clues to what he was scribbling.

I raised my shoulders after spilling the beans. "What do you think?"

"The short answer: yes, Judge Hoffman will have to recuse herself if you hire me." He assured me I had a temporary way out of trial.

I let out a sigh of relief.

"But before I can agree to take on the case, I need to run some names by my partners. There may be conflicts of interest here," he cautioned.

I panicked as he got up and left the room. *Please, God, this is my only chance,* I prayed. *Please let him agree to do it.* I was prepared to beg.

I needed to calm myself, so I got silly with Phoebe. She giggled as I sang songs and danced Big Bird around on her tray. She held up Cookie Monster for me to dance him around too. She roared with laughter as my trembling hands made the figurines dance wildly about.

"Okay, we're good," Bruce said as he walked back in.

I looked up to the sky. *Thank you.* I smiled at Phoebe. *We're going to be okay, baby*, I thought as I kissed her on the head.

"Don't retain me today. I'd have to let all parties know I represent you," he explained. "That would give them time to put the trial before another judge."

I nodded.

"I say lay low, and see what happens," Bruce advised. "Maybe your ex will get hit by a bus."

"I wish." I wasn't kidding.

"If not, retain me the night before trial. We'll surprise them in court. Catch them off guard." Bruce winked. He seemed to enjoy his plan.

"Sounds good to me," I said, as if I liked Bruce's plan too. My mind spun in a dark orbit of things that could go wrong. An unforeseen event could throw a wrench in the plan, or Bruce could change his mind and abandon me. I desperately wanted to retain him that instant and have him fix everything on the spot. But I restrained myself from pushing, out of fear I might push too hard and be left standing alone.

~

The lull in the drama over the next couple of months captivated me like the calm before a storm. I was determined to put a nonreactive mindset into practice and train myself to handle life with dignity. I created a folder in my inbox labeled "Need to Respond—Eventually" and filed Jason's incessant emails away. I stood patiently behind Phoebe's stroller, waiting for the boys, while Jason put on a show of affection at school doors, sporting events, and plays. I'd freeze for a moment if I saw a car parked outside my house but then ask myself, "What's the worst that could happen?" I tolerated the real estate agent who paraded potential buyers in and out of my house for appointments. In some ways, it seemed like I didn't care about anything anymore, but I just didn't care to waste my energy. I tried to stay centered in the storm, pray, and trust the outcome. None of this was natural for me; it was more like "fake it 'til you make it."

In December, less than a month before trial, Abe called to set up a meeting with Jason and me to try one last attempt at mediation. No attorneys would be present; he wanted to talk to us alone. Jason and I arrived at the same time and sat awkwardly across from each other in the waiting room. I was hopeful but guarded. Jason seemed annoyed to be there, checking his watch and fidgeting in his seat. I remembered how it agitated him to do things that didn't serve his agenda. Normally, I would have played meek to placate him, or twitched with anxiety anticipating the next blow. But I was realizing that I possessed a strength that required no action.

Abe gathered us into his office and tried to lighten the tension. He situated three chairs so that he was directly across from me and Jason, as opposed to behind his desk. He seemed more like a grandfather or yogi master instead of the court-appointed lawyer for the children. I let my guard down, ready to hear him impart his wisdom. It was like I'd gone on a mission, reached the end, and was ready to go home. I wanted to say, "I'm done. Show me the way."

Jason sat bent forward with his legs spread wide apart, his elbows propped on his knees, and his chin cupped in one hand like *The Thinker* sculpture. It was an overexaggerated pose of feigned interest in what Abe had to say.

"The boys are really great kids," Abe began. "Time flies. You're going to regret wasting so much of it in conflict." He was trying to tell us to let all the anger go. "Don't be so focused on the schedule; focus on the quality of your time," he advised. "Be with the kids—really be with them." Suddenly the color-coded calendar I'd drafted seemed foolish. "Before you know it, they'll be grown and living according to their own schedules. You're going to want them to want to be around you," Abe cautioned.

I cringed at the times I had created tension in my home because of my hatred toward Jason. My relationship with my boys mattered more than winning this war.

Jason hung on every word and nodded like he too was taking it all in. But I could feel his refusal to soften or weaken. I could feel his hatred so strongly that I couldn't tell where my energy ended and his began. An inner struggle erupted between my desire for peace and my commitment to war. The need for vengeance bubbled inside me.

"Maybe, instead of trial, you can work out some kinks in the agreement. Come to terms and enjoy life, enjoy the kids," Abe suggested, boosting my desire for peace.

"I'd be happy to do that," I jumped in, eager to dispel my hate.

"I'd like some time to think about everything," Jason slyly said.

Abe encouraged a settlement. "Okay, and then have Nick call Francesca to work something out."

Jason patronized Abe. "Absolutely."

Abe had done his part. The rest was up to us. Jason and I walked out in the same direction toward our cars.

I made a guarded attempt to strike a deal. "Okay then, so I guess I'll be hearing from Nick?"

"Sure." Jason smirked.

I knew I would need Bruce. I eventually called to tell him Abe had encouraged us to settle, but that I never heard from Nick. I'd even tried Nick myself, but he never returned my call. Bruce wasn't in deep enough to be affected, but I could tell he didn't appreciate jerks. He wanted to help me. I retained him the night before the trial. I was ready, not because I wanted to win, but because I wanted to live.

The next morning, I slowly dressed for court like I was getting ready to attend my own funeral. I had a peculiar sense that I was going to witness some sort of end to me. Trial would be postponed for a while, then eventually go on—like when a loved one dies and life stops for a while, but then goes on, differently.

I walked through the metal detectors, determined not to make eye contact with anyone, paranoid about giving off any clues of my escape. A top-secret attorney and a closet real estate listing were in place. I couldn't risk having anyone on to me who might thwart my plan. All this drama, but meanwhile, the blocks to my freedom were all in my mind. I was the only one in my way.

I sat in the waiting area with my head down, aware that Jason was already there. I was afraid if he noticed any hint of relief in me, he would interfere with my plan. Unable to help myself, I anxiously peeked up through my bangs and saw him reading a book titled, *How to Win at Gambling*. I don't know what I found more shocking, the fact that he was so disconnected from the trial, or that he would openly read a gambling manual while trying to win custody.

Nick arrived, and Jason jumped from his seat to pat him on the back. His enthusiasm at having Nick at his disposal made my stomach turn. Nick shot me a nasty look. I guess he didn't appreciate the pending corruption investigations I'd initiated.

I let out a deep breath when Bruce walked in. He breezed through the waiting room like a VIP and nodded at me, reassuring me that all was proceeding according to plan. Nick caught the exchange, and I could tell something clicked in his mind. Jason, on the other hand, smiled like a dope. He had no clue who Bruce was.

Bruce whispered to the officer standing guard over Hoffman's courtroom. The officer shook his head in acknowledgment and opened the door to allow Bruce entry. A few minutes later, a plump secretary emerged, and Nick was called in. Jason looked a bit confused by the lack of protocol but seemed game for whatever was about to go down. He looked at me, hoping, I presumed, to get pleasure from my anxiety.

I sat still and prayed.

It felt like an eternity, but moments later the door swung open and Bruce barged out. "Trial's off," he announced.

Nick followed behind Bruce. Jason's head snapped from Bruce to Nick.

"She's smarter than you," Nick said.

He ushered Jason to a quiet corner to fill him in on the turn of events. Jason raised his arms and covered the sides of his head, rocking back and forth in disbelief. He bent over like he'd been kicked in the gut and moved his hands to his knees. Without his cronies lined up, his case was meaningless. He looked so pathetic, I was embarrassed for him. What had I been afraid of?

We were all called into the courtroom so Judge Hoffman could recuse herself on the record. Abe was called over the loudspeaker. He made his way in and smiled at Bruce.

"Counsel, it was brought to the attention of the court this morning that the defendant retained Mr. Gentile to represent her," Judge Hoffman began. "Due to a personal conflict of inter-est with Mr. Gentile, I need to recuse myself from this case." She looked at Bruce as if to say, "Touché."

Bruce nodded. They had played this game before.

I walked out of the courtroom feeling empowered. I would need Bruce by my side for a while, but eventually I'd be able to proceed on my own. We walked together confidently down the hall and left Jason raging behind. A chill ran up my spine as I sensed demons blazing behind me, but I didn't dare look back. I had to let them melt away while I kept walking. With each step, I felt a layer of anguish shed from me. As the layers shed, I discovered glimmers of myself. Francesca was still there.

chapter twenty-six

THE ROAD TO RECOVERY IS PAVED WITH TWO STEPS FORWARD and one step back. That's how the next several months of the custody battle, and life, played out.

Our case was reassigned to Judge Nancy Beck, a retired judge who was called back to the bench to help manage an overwhelming caseload in our county. As a retiree, she had no political agenda, and Bruce reassured me it would be a fair trial. In some ways that comforted me, but at the same time, it triggered my paranoia. If she ruled in favor of Jason, then my corruption allegations would be unfounded, making me the monster after all.

I stood at attention in the courtroom at our first appearance before Judge Beck. Her stern voice and scolding temperament made up for her petite stature and bony features. "This case has been before the court long enough, Counsel. I'm setting trial for May." She looked at her calendar and called out some dates. "I want an updated forensics report by then," she ordered. "The parties need to cooperate and schedule appointments with—" She looked down at the file. "Dr. David Levine."

Ugh, Levine again, I thought.

I made the obligatory call to Levine later that afternoon. I cringed at the sound of his voice on the answering machine and left a brief message requesting an appointment.

I never heard back from Levine. Before I knew it, we were

back in court for a status appearance with Judge Beck. Jason appeared subdued as he filed into her courtroom. Nick wasn't with him. *That's strange*, I thought, as Bruce and Abe and I took our places.

"Dr. Levine isn't able to update the forensics report due to a family tragedy," Judge Beck began. "I reassigned the case to Dr. Rachel Katz. She'll need some time to conduct her evaluation. Trial will be pushed to the first week of October."

I can't keep enduring more months of this, I thought as I tried to quickly process the news. *But maybe time is good; maybe it will go away. Maybe I can come up with a way out.* My mind raced. *I wonder what Bruce knows about Dr. Katz.* I made a note to ask him. I also wondered what had happened to Levine—and to Nick.

"Mr. Axcel, you're here without representation today?" Beck scowled at Jason.

"Yes, Your Honor," Jason submissively replied.

"I trust you will have representation at trial?" She looked over the rim of her glasses.

"Yes, Your Honor." He sounded shaky. "I'm in the process of retaining an attorney."

Interesting, I thought.

"I'll see you all back at trial." She dismissed us for the day.

~

I had an appointment with my therapist not long after the appearance. I was seeing Angela regularly. Ironically, she had office space right down the hall from Dr. Levine.

"What happened to Levine?" I asked after we settled in. I was curious about his family tragedy.

Angela looked confused.

"He took himself off the case because of a family tragedy," I explained. I'd assumed she already knew.

"He's been working his regular schedule." She raised an eyebrow. "There was no family tragedy I'm aware of."

This validated my theory that something fishy was at play, which agitated me even more. I'd been tormented by these bullies, who got to run away while I still had to endure the case. I spent the session spewing my anger and venting about how screwed up everyone was.

I got temporary relief from raging aloud, but soon after my session, my head was thick with stories of past transgressions. The mental retelling of wrongdoings drained me. I hated how I felt, and I feared I would have a breakdown. I forced myself to pretend to the outside world that the drama was behind me. I don't know if I was trying to help myself or clear my image, or both.

No matter how hard I tried, I couldn't live happily with a tormented mind. Socializing at school events and birthday parties drained me. I despised suburbia and dreaded the effort involved in maintaining friendships. My shoulders slumped when I received the invitation to an '80s themed fortieth birthday party at a friend's house in Queens. My mind raced with excuses to get out of it, but it was for one of my closest friends. We had to go.

"Why aren't we dressing '80s style?" Theo asked as we got ready the night of the party.

"I'm not dressing up." I sounded like a defiant toddler. I didn't enjoy theme parties. The last thing I wanted to do was relive the past.

We walked into a room filled with guests in neon outfits and teased hair, laughing over shots of Woo Woo. I immediately felt out of place; I always did. I stood in a corner with a drink in my hand, awkwardly trying to manage a small appetizer plate in the other.

"Frannie! How are you?" Matt, a guy from Queens I had known since I was a teenager, asked as he walked over.

"Doing well. How about you?" I shifted from foot to foot, anxious as I fought to make small talk.

"Good, thanks." He looked me over. "You look nice." My modern dress and sleek blowout were in sharp contrast to his acid-washed denim. I half-smiled and nodded.

"I saw Mr. Axcel not too long ago." My entire body tensed at Matt's mention of my ex. But something about the formal reference indicated Matt wanted to disassociate from him.

"Did you?" My interest was piqued.

"He sounded brokenhearted about you two splitting up," he added as if he sensed my curiosity.

"Please! That's such bullshit." I scoffed. "He's suing me for custody. Trust me, he's not brokenhearted. He has no heart." My anger was poked.

Matt commiserated. "You know, Frannie, I sensed he was full of it. He was practically crying fake tears."

"Where did you see him?" I asked.

"At a fundraiser." He paused. "I don't know if you heard, I'm running for office out east," he boasted.

"You might not want to associate with Jason and his cronies," I warned. "They're all going down one day." As much as I longed for peace, I couldn't move on without vindication. I sounded like a fool and I knew it, but I couldn't help myself. The case remained at the forefront of my life, no matter how hard I battled to make it disappear. Matt looked at me as if to say, "Go on."

"I'm getting away from him and Prospect Isle politics," I added, forcing myself to sound like I was beyond the anger. "My new husband and I are moving to New Jersey." I glanced over at Theo to prove I had moved on.

We had recently put an offer in on a traditional colonial in a garden-variety town. The aesthetic inspired me to be an apple pie suburban mom with a coiffed bob and a tennis club demeanor. I was so desperate for a fresh start, I was willing to sell my soul to the PTA.

"Jersey? Really?" Matt seemed to soak up the information. "What part?" he asked.

"Wyckoff. I can go fifty miles away from that ass, and it just about gets me there." I was hesitant to make a move, but Theo was adamant. "Jason can drive over bridges if he wants to see his kids." I bragged about my power even though Bruce had warned me not to make a move until after trial.

"I hope it all works out." Matt flashed a sly smile and excused himself to the bar.

He left me standing alone, stewing in misery. Celebratory laughter filled the room around me, but the intoxicated adults deepened my depression. I wasn't quite sure what had just happened, but whatever it was, I was certain it forecasted more doom.

~

Later that week, I sat on a couch across from Dr. Rachel Katz to start my new forensics evaluation. I couldn't help but take stock of her, even though she was supposed to assess me. She seemed around my age, almost forty. She sat on the couch with one leg crossed under the other, and seemed more like a teenage girl than a doctor. We exchanged pleasantries, and then her cell phone rang.

"Excuse me, I have to take this." She held up her pointer finger while she answered. "Is everything okay? Are you feeling okay?" she said into the phone. After a beat, she added, "I won't be too long today. Don't answer the door or anything—just stay on the couch and watch TV."

She focused her attention back on me. "Sorry about that. I left my daughter home alone sick from school today," she explained. "She's ten, she's fine—but if she calls again, I'll have to answer."

She's ten, sick, and home alone, I thought. *This woman is evaluating me?* I was tempted to get up from the couch and march out the door. But fear of ruffling feathers forced me to stay put. And so began another psychological evaluation of my family and me. A stranger was put in charge of judging me and telling the court what was best for my boys.

I composed myself until I turned out of her parking lot, but once I was out of the judgment zone, I pressed my foot on the gas. *Who the hell was this woman to be in charge of my life?* I fumed. The freedom of the road and the power of the wheel inspired me to take control of something in my life. The New Jersey apple pie house was *not* for me. I rolled my eyes at the thought of living in a cookie-cutter town surrounded by white picket fences and Stepford wives.

"I was thinking," I said to Theo later that evening, "I don't really want to live in New Jersey. I don't think it's the house for us after all." I casually dropped a heavy conversation bomb while he sat in his recliner watching TV.

"What are you talking about?" he asked without taking his

eyes off his show. "You love that house." He didn't want to deal with my overactive mind.

"Yeah, the house is pretty, but honestly, who wants all that space?" I replied, but he wasn't convinced. "Plus there's work to be done in that basement, and I didn't really like how many steps there were down to the yard." I babbled, because I didn't know how to articulate my desire to roam free, to have no boundaries, to live unrestrained. "Plus I was researching the commute. It's at least ninety minutes to your office on a good day. Do you really want to be dealing with that?" I knew he hated commuting.

"Fine." He finally agreed, disgusted. "But we're not staying here."

The next day, Theo rescinded the offer on the Jersey house and wasted no time setting up appointments in Westchester. We house hunted every other weekend with Phoebe in tow while the boys were with Jason. I didn't want to waste our family weekends sitting in traffic. I was so fearful of losing precious family time, I put undue pressure on us all to make the most of the time we did have. Anything less than a perfect day together roused debilitating sadness in me. I was paranoid that a bad day meant I was failing my kids and that in the long run, we'd be a broken family.

House hunting in a new area without the boys stirred gloom, forewarning a life without them under my roof. I leaned my forehead on the glass and gazed out the passenger window as Theo drove through winding roads filled with unfamiliar, yet familiar, homes. Suburbia was suburbia—nothing would change but the cast of characters. I didn't want to move to another suburb and complicate life further. The problem was, I didn't know what I wanted. I couldn't put my finger on it. I felt it but couldn't speak it in tangible terms.

I was lost in a fog of house hunting and uncertainty for a few weeks until I was jolted by another family court envelope in my mail. I trembled as I opened it, paranoid about what they could possibly want now. We didn't have an appearance on the calendar until the October trial. I couldn't believe my eyes. Jason had filed a motion to have me restrained to town, or give up temporary custody of the boys. I was ordered to appear before the court in a couple of days.

I frantically dialed Bruce.

"Did you see the order?" I asked, shaking.

"I told you to wait until after the trial," he scolded.

My head hung heavy with shame for disappointing him. I feared he'd view me as flawed and refuse to represent me any longer.

"We canceled that Jersey contract," I reminded him. "We're technically not moving anywhere at the moment. We have our house on the market because we need another bedroom."

"I'll see you in court," he said dourly. "Oh, take a look at who prepared the order . . . his new attorney is a shark," he added just before he hung up.

chapter twenty-seven

I WAS NUMB WITH FEAR AS I WAITED TO BE CALLED INTO Judge Beck's courtroom. Bruce sat next to me but barely said a word to me. Jason was accompanied by a large, mob-like lawyer, whom I presumed was Vincent Scarpella, the attorney who had prepared the motion. We took our places in the courtroom, and I forced myself to stand straight even though my knees trembled.

"The matter before the court today is a motion seeking to restrain the defendant to her current town, or have her give up temporary custody of the children," Judge Beck began. A chill ran up my spine.

"Counsel?" she said to Bruce.

"Your Honor, my client has a right to live anywhere within fifty miles of the children's father," Bruce replied. "There's no basis for this hearing."

"Your Honor," Scarpella interrupted, "the defendant is *ripping* the children from their father and their childhood town in the middle of a custody case!" He screamed as he waved pictures of my house listing in the air like he had caught me red-handed. I felt violated by his invasion of my privacy. I later learned he'd subpoenaed the real estate broker for details of my private listing. The agent never had the decency to tell me.

Scarpella tried to expose me for the horrible person Jason claimed I was. "We have reason to believe she's moving to New

Jersey to put undue strain on my client's ability to see his children!"

My jaw clenched as I recalled the conversation I'd had with Matt at the fortieth birthday party. I was sure he'd ratted me out. I was so adamant about exposing Jason that night and clearing my own name, I'd screwed myself.

"Your Honor," Bruce jumped in, "my client and her husband are selling their house simply because they need more space. She's looking for a home well within the fifty-mile parameter of the divorce agreement."

"There's no crime in listing a house for sale," Beck said to Scarpella as she looked over some papers on her desk. "According to the agreement, the defendant does have the right to move within a fifty-mile radius. I won't issue an immediate restraining order or temporary change in custody today. I'll issue a written decision on the matter after I've had some time to review. In the meantime, the parties should follow the agreement and make decisions in the best interest of the children."

I let out a huge sigh of relief as if I had just had a big win, but Bruce rushed from the courtroom like he was trying to get away from me.

"See, she realizes I can technically go fifty miles," I said as I hurried to keep up with him. "This was a total waste of our time." I tried to convince him I wasn't doing anything wrong.

"I still wouldn't move forward if I were you," he advised.

"Why?" I protested.

"Just wait." He gave fair warning before he rushed ahead to his next case.

I stormed out of the building, fed up with Jason and family court and irritated by Bruce's restrictive advice. His dismissiveness triggered resentment with myself for being submissive. I was so determined to have my own way that I refused to hear his sound advice.

"The judge agreed we have fifty miles." I called Theo from the car with my defiant interpretation of the facts.

"Great!" he exclaimed.

We accepted a pending offer on our house and went right back to searching in Westchester as a blatant flip off to Jason and his case. We found a colonial on a cul-de-sac in a desirable neighborhood, with good schools and easy access to midtown Manhattan. Theo excitedly inspected the house and proudly negotiated a deal. I was desperate for a fresh start. Moving was the only way that seemed possible. I didn't understand that the change needed to come from within. I convinced myself I was excited about the house, but I was still grasping at something I couldn't quite identify.

Later that week, I drove through our town to pick the boys up from playdates. They were each with friends in a hamlet where a lot of young families lived. I grabbed Ben first and then made my way over to get Gavin. Phoebe giggled and clapped her hands when Ben hopped in the car. The air had a slight April chill, and the sky was beginning its ebb from daylight to dark. It reminded me of childhood nights in Queens, when neighborhood kids played stickball or manhunt until dinner. Ben energetically chatted away about how much fun he'd had at Katie's, and his happiness warmed my soul.

I pulled up to Evan's and slowly steered around several bicycles lined up at the curb. Basketballs, footballs, and bike helmets were strewn about. Gavin and several boys were running around the front lawn playing touch football. My heart swelled at the sight of Gavin's happy-go-lucky smile. I rolled down the window to call him, and through a hazy, dreamlike state, I transformed into my mother, looking out the window of her yellow station wagon many decades before. I recalled a warm longing in her eyes that now sparked in me. It dawned on me that she too had yearned to harness the very thing I desperately wanted: happiness.

~

I spent the next few weeks moving about gently, breathing slowly, trying to hold onto that feeling so it wouldn't escape me. I worried that once we moved, I'd have to start all over to find it again. I feared I wouldn't be able to, or worse, I'd discover that what I'd been looking for had been back in our old house. I didn't know how to explain the sensation to Theo in a way he would understand. How could I explain that I wanted a feeling, not a house? I continued to pack and move forward while I obsessively checked the mail for Beck's order regarding the move, like I was searching for a message on a scroll.

When the manila envelope finally arrived one Saturday afternoon, I tore it open with anticipation and dread. We were ordered to stay put until after the custody trial, which meant I couldn't move until at least several months after we were scheduled to close on both homes. The judge took the position that if I moved the boys and settled them into a new town and school, it would impede the court's ability to rule in favor of the dad and disrupt the boys yet again. I wanted to obey her order, not only because I didn't want to hurt my chances at trial, but because it felt like she'd sent me a message: *moving is not how you fix it.*

I inhaled momentary relief before I tensed again at the thought of showing Theo. I knew he would flip out.

"The, uh, the judge's order came in the mail just now," I stammered.

He grabbed the order from my hands and read it quickly, then slammed it down onto the kitchen counter and stormed out the door.

"Where are you going?" I pleaded from the driveway.

"Out!" He drove off.

Trembling, I called my brother Dominick.

"Fuck the order!" he exclaimed. "Let Theo close on the house, and you and the kids can move there right after trial." It seemed like a no-brainer to him.

His advice made sense, but I didn't want to take the risk. I knew it appeared I wasn't brave enough, but I instinctively sensed I shouldn't fight the current. I suddenly felt calm, centered, clear.

A few hours later, Theo came home. I could tell from his light movements that he wasn't as angry as when he left. He must have sensed a glow in me, a peace that radiated from my soul, because he hugged me, and I melted into him.

"I still want to sell this house." He filled me in on his thoughts from his drive. "We need more space," he reasoned. I sensed he wanted to find a place together that he'd had a say in choosing. I could empathize with his need for a voice. "But we can find one locally." This put me at ease.

I called a real estate agent about a house that was for sale in the neighborhood where I'd felt happiness the night I picked up the boys from playdates. We met her there for a quick tour, but it wasn't the house for us.

She called me a few days later. "You're not going to believe this. A couple walked in today to list the exact house you described wanting, on the exact block you want to be on!" She couldn't believe it herself. "It's not hitting the market until next week, but they'll allow you to preview it."

We met her there Sunday afternoon. It was just right. We wasted no time making an offer and scheduled a follow-up appointment for an inspection later that week. We all enthusiastically went back for another peek at the house. Gavin and Ben eagerly claimed their bedrooms, and Phoebe played on the swing set in the yard. The boys ran through the finished basement, buzzing with anticipation of the fun they would have there.

I corralled the kids for a walk so Theo and the engineer could focus on the inspection. I pointed out the charming street signs that adorned each corner, as if we were moving to Storybook Land. The boys were wide-eyed as they counted the number of friends' houses we passed and realized how easy it would be to see them every day. I assumed the new house brought us happiness, but now I think my desire for happiness brought us the new house.

The better I felt, the more peaceful life became. Even forensics didn't seem like part of a battle to me. It felt more like a safe haven than a court-appointed evaluation. Dr. Katz was relatable, and I was able to be authentic with her. She didn't use her power to stir up drama; she seemed to want to get to the root of the problem and solve it.

The boys also seemed at ease in sessions that included them. At one session, they were in the middle of a game when my phone rang. I didn't pick up at first, but it kept ringing and ringing in my bag.

"It's Jason," I explained to Dr. Katz as I grabbed the phone from my bag.

"You can take it," she said. "It seems urgent."

"Is something wrong?" I said as I answered. "I'm at a forensics session with the boys."

"I'd like to talk to them," he requested coldly.

"They're in the middle of a session," I repeated.

"Fran, let me talk to the boys," he demanded.

"Guys, Daddy wants to talk." I handed them the phone as I shrugged at Dr. Katz.

"He has no boundaries," she huffed.

～

A week or so later, I relaxed on Dr. Katz's couch for my last session. She casually asked some wrap-up questions to help finalize her report. The mood was light, and I felt optimistic about the direction life might be heading.

"Jason told me you tried to move, but the judge stopped it?" she asked.

Here we go again. I was tired of endless scrutiny.

She prompted me to explain. "What was that about?"

"I don't know," I said, sighing. "I just couldn't take it anymore." It was too broad a statement. She waited for more.

"I wasn't comfortable living in a town controlled by Jason and his corrupt cronies." The injustice of it all seemed enough explanation to me, but she didn't seem satisfied with my answer.

"There's a constant police presence outside my house, and it rattles me to be served in front of my kids." I was tired of chaos and drama, and angry I couldn't escape it. "Every time I walk out my door, my skin crawls and I look over my shoulder, feeling stalked. Every move I make is documented." I was riddled with unwarranted guilt and paranoid about being less than perfect.

Dr. Katz nodded.

"Part of me wanted to punish him." I felt justified in saying so. I'd been caught in a rip current of negative emotions and frantically swimming to fight it, unable to save myself. Frustrated, I lashed out at others.

Dr. Katz looked at me like she knew I knew better.

Would that really make me happy?

"I wanted a clean slate. I wanted to live life freely." Relief filled my lungs as I spoke the words out loud.

She smiled.

"We're staying put," I reassured her.

She nodded and jotted down some notes.

"I just don't know how to get this nightmare out of my life," I revealed. I was worn out and in despair, but I held out hope for a better way.

"Today's session concludes my evaluation." Dr. Katz changed gears. Her warm eyes indicated she saw the raw me, the broken girl, the abused young lady, the devoted mother, the fierce woman. I guessed she saw the real Jason too.

"I'd like to talk to you off the record." She turned off her recorder, put down her notepad, and sat cross-legged in her chair. "Do you realize Jason is a sociopath?"

"C'mon." I was taken aback. "I mean, he's crazy, but he's not roaming the streets murdering people." I was actually sticking up for him.

"Sociopaths don't necessarily murder people, although some do," she explained. "They're more likely to use mind games to control and manipulate a chosen target."

Okay, this I could buy. I shifted in my seat, sitting up a bit straighter and leaning in toward her so I didn't miss anything.

"They're often charismatic and charming," she went on.

I recalled my dating years with Jason, how he'd charmed my friends and me, and how later he'd charmed the PTA moms. It's also how he portrayed himself in the political arena.

"A sociopath doesn't have a conscience. They'll do anything and use any means to get what they want," Dr. Katz explained.

No wonder he had no problem using the boys as weapons in his war against me.

"They enjoy watching their target suffer," she added.

I pictured Jason's smirk and shuddered at the memory of his sadistic laugh.

"They show no remorse. Court battles are common for them."

How had I missed this?

"Ironically, at one of our sessions, he accused you of being one," she added.

My head snapped back. This news confirmed how detached he was and how much he wanted to destroy me.

"Read *The Sociopath Next Door*," she advised. "It'll explain it all and give you tools for how to deal with him. In fact, the best way to deal with him is *not* to deal with him," she added, in case I didn't read it.

I wondered how it would be possible to detach from him. I feared that if I kept myself and the boys away from him, he'd come at me harder, and I'd lose them to his grip.

She tipped me off. "I'm going to write a report that will no doubt get you out of court. Litigation is his favorite tool for torture," she acknowledged. "But he will try other methods," she warned.

What else would he do? I shivered. *How could I protect myself and my family?*

As if she had heard my questions, she said, "You need to calmly disengage. Stop showing fear or anger. In fact, show no emotions at all. Be totally dull. He'll get bored with you, and, unfortunately for them, move on to another target," she said as if she were looking into a crystal ball.

I had the power to not be his victim anymore. Dr. Katz would get me out of court hell—the rest was up to me.

"In time, he'll have no relationship with the boys. I say give it six or seven years, and he'll be out of your lives."

She looked at her watch, indicating time was just about up. "Well, that's all from me. Any questions?"

I shook my head. I was still processing everything she'd told me. "Thank you so much," I said, not knowing what else to say.

"Take care," she said. "I hope it all works out for you."

Filled with hope, I walked out to my car. Not only had she shared how she would handle the report, she'd armed me with knowledge that I possessed power after all.

chapter twenty-eight

•

I KEPT THE DETAILS OF THE LAST FORENSICS SESSION TO MYSELF, not wanting to diminish the intrigue. I read the book Dr. Katz recommended and was blown away by how much I related to it, by how easily I'd allowed myself to be a victim. I methodically packed the house, as I inwardly contemplated all that I learned. I wanted this all out of my life.

My phone rang, and I could tell from the caller ID it was the district attorney's office. I hadn't heard from them in a while, and I'd lost touch with the status of the investigation. I feared it had fizzled out, but I'd been afraid to check in and find out.

"Ms. Panagos? It's Ed Donolan from the DA's office." Ed was my main contact there.

"Hi, Mr. Donolan." My stomach dropped.

"I'm calling to let you know we wrapped up our investigation. We're going to have to close the case."

"How is that possible?" I asked. "They're just going to get away with it?" I flung my free hand in the air.

"The call tape isn't clear enough. We just don't have a smoking gun," he explained.

I stared into space, frustrated that no one in power understood my plight. "I guess there's nothing else I can do," I said dismissively. As much as I wanted vindication, I wanted the drama out of my life more. I put my faith in Dr. Katz's pending report.

"We've been working closely with the FBI," he added. "They're closing out on their end too."

It was a tough pill to swallow. Years later, the Feds nailed the town politicians for corruption unrelated to my case. I watched Jason and his fellow thugs finally fall from grace. People in my close circle reveled in the news. My phone rang off the hook the day it hit the press. I enjoyed the satisfaction, but I didn't harp on it. I found more pleasure from feeling content with my own life.

I did my best to will the case behind me as we moved into our new house in the summer of 2010. The boys were with Jason the weekend of the move, so I used the time to nest in anticipation of their arrival at their new home. Their bedroom furniture was situated, their clothes neatly tucked away. Beds were made, wall decor hung, and favorite mementos placed on shelves. The playroom was in order, the refrigerator stocked, the pantry filled with snacks. I unpacked with tireless determination to give them a more stable life as I prayed that my family would find peace.

Theo and the kids settled into the new house and life in the hamlet with ease and joy. I walked around like a deer in headlights, living on the brink of a breakdown. I forced a smile through clenched teeth, constantly praying, *please make the case go away. Please don't take my kids from me and this happy home. Please make it stop.*

Trial date was approaching, and we were anxiously waiting for the report. Every morning I stared at the feng shui symbol the prior homeowner had left above the front door in the entry hall. "I'm going to leave this for you," she said the day she gave us the keys. "It's meant to keep legal problems out of your life," she gently explained. I barely knew her through mutual acquaintances in town, but I guess she'd heard my story. She didn't judge; she showed empathy. I hoped to be that kind to others. Every day, I looked at that ornament with hope and trust that the case would go away.

~

I was sipping my coffee and about to clean up after breakfast one morning when my phone rang.

"The report's ready," Bruce said. "I'm on my way to court to read it now."

My heart skipped a beat. I was one step away from potentially life-altering news.

Bruce filled my silence. "Abe and Scarpella are on their way too."

Three attorneys were on their way to assess the situation and would know the fate of my family before I did. They'd deliver the news. The severity of it paralyzed me.

"Sit tight. I'll call you when we're done." Bruce hung up.

I inhaled as much air as my lungs could hold. I watched my kids move about the house and the yard like they were optical illusions. I wasn't sure if they would ultimately take form or vanish. I murmured a desperate, begging kind of prayer for the next couple of hours.

My heart jumped when Bruce finally called. I picked up on the first ring.

I answered with an urgent plea. "Bruce?"

"It's over. Your ex doesn't have a leg to stand on."

I exhaled years of trauma and dropped to my knees, humbled by the mercy of a force that was far beyond the courts.

Bruce shared some bits about the report, but I was too excited to process the details. All I could understand was that Dr. Katz had done exactly what she'd promised. Jason was portrayed in a rather unfavorable light, and his claim for custody was deemed completely unwarranted.

"What happens now?" I asked as I steadied myself against the kitchen table.

"We'll have to settle on some modifications to the divorce agreement. Maybe give him an extra dinner night or an extra overnight during the month," Bruce explained.

"*What?*" I shrieked. "Why the hell would I give him more time? Shouldn't he have to *give up* time?" I was appalled.

Bruce let me unload.

"Shouldn't he be paying my legal fees? Shouldn't I be able to sue *him* for false accusations?" I asked, outraged.

Bruce laid it out. "Look, he's never going to just drop the case. He'd rather fight the forensics report in trial than walk away with nothing. His attorney plans to let him know the report is heavily stacked against him. They'll demand certain changes on his behalf, and we'll agree to make him feel as if he got something after all." Bruce tried to reason and get me to see it was my ticket to freedom from Jason and the court battle.

"If settling means I get to live in peace, then fine," I agreed.

"I'll make sure to get things fixed for you too," Bruce promised. "Summer vacation language and Mother's Day and Christmas Eve." He knew the drill.

"Seems like a lot of time and money and agony to modify a few terms that could have been handled in a meeting." I boiled with anger and resentment. I would never get back the years I'd spent tormented by the case, never mind the hundreds of thousands in legal fees.

"And look, you're keeping full custody. That's a big deal. In the end, this guy still has no claim to his own kids." Bruce tried to help me look on the bright side.

True. He won't be able to control and manipulate them.

"Oh, one more thing," Bruce casually added. "You need to agree to stay in town until the boys are eighteen."

"So now I'm on house arrest?" I quipped.

"You just bought the house. I'm sure you're staying. By the time you're ready to move again, the boys will be older and probably won't have anything to do with him anyway." He was right, but I resented Jason's continued influence over my life and my freedom.

I took the boys for ice cream to fill them in.

"Why do we have to change the dinner schedule?" Gavin asked, confused by what that had to do with anything.

"I don't want to stay over an extra night on Dad's weekends," Ben whined.

Hadn't anyone heard them?

"These are just some little things we're going to do so Mommy doesn't have to go to court anymore. Hopefully there won't be any more fighting or cops or video cameras or doctor appointments." I tried to convince them it was for the best, but I couldn't help but feel I had failed them. None of it had been their fault, but they were burdened with the responsibility of adjusting to it. They both shrugged in acceptance as they scraped the last of the ice cream from their cups.

~

On October 5, 2010, I walked through metal detectors for what I hoped would be the last time. I made eye contact with the guard, looking for him to acknowledge this was it. Jason showed up with a female attorney who was handling the wrap-up for Scarpella. (Jason wasn't paying his bills on time, and the head shark didn't want to waste any more time on him.) My legs trembled as I sat on a bench while she, Bruce, and Abe were called into the judge's chambers. My heart raced and my palms sweat as I stared at the closed door, anticipating Bruce would barge out and tell me trial was back on. Everything up to that point was such an unbelievable nightmare, I couldn't trust it would ever end.

The door swung open and the attorneys filed out like they'd just seen a ghost. Bruce took a seat next to me and let out a sigh. "Your ex does *not* want to settle."

My heart dropped. "Now what?"

"Too bad for him. It's getting settled," he assured me.

"How can you be sure?" My head swirled with panic.

"We all took care of it in chambers. I never heard Abe curse about someone like that before." Bruce wiped his brow. "Your ex's attorney is speaking to him now. She knows he's a bastard." He straightened his tie.

Moments later, she approached Bruce. "Can you help me explain the terms to my client?" She pursed her lips.

"What?" Bruce was baffled.

"He's impossible," she pleaded.

Bruce walked toward Jason, and for a moment I thought they'd come to blows. Jason was shouting demands, but he was powerless without his cronies. Bruce did not back down. He said what he had to say and walked away, leaving Jason dumbfounded.

"What a prick," Bruce exclaimed.

We were finally called before the judge and sworn in.

Okay, it's moving along. I took deep breaths. *One step closer to freedom.*

"Good afternoon to the parties and counsel," Judge Beck began. "I understand that a resolution has been reached in the matter. Who is going to put that on the record?"

"With Your Honor's permission, I will," Bruce said. He proceeded to detail exactly what he'd promised the settlement would be. Jason's attorney added a note of clarity to a point or two, simply doing her job.

Judge Beck marked the case settled, and by way of formality had to ask the parties if they understood and agreed to the settlement terms.

She addressed Jason first. "Mr. Axcel, have you heard what has been placed on the record today?" I held my breath. *Almost at the finish line.*

"Yes, Your Honor." Jason's voice was soft, like he didn't want to acknowledge defeat.

"You understand all the terms and conditions?" she asked.

"Yes, Your Honor." Anger crept into his words.

"No one has forced or coerced you to consent to these terms?" Beck confirmed.

"No, Your Honor, no," he replied through flared nostrils. I'd seen that look before. It was over for now, but he wasn't done.

No way. I'll never allow it again, I vowed to myself.

Judge Beck turned to me. "Mrs. Panagos, have you heard what has been placed on the record today?"

"Yes, Your Honor." I cringed with shame for being in this mess in the first place.

"You understand all the terms and conditions?" she asked.

"Yes, Your Honor." I wished they knew how smart I was.

"No one has forced or coerced you to consent to these terms?" Judge Beck was about to tap her gavel.

Are you kidding me? I thought. All I had to do was agree and it would be over, but I yearned to speak out. *Of course I was forced and coerced. What choice did I have to put an end to my suffering? My ex is dangerous, and the court indulged him instead of protecting my boys and me. You made me the bad guy and coddled his so-called rights while dragging me and my family through years of torture. No one listened to me. No one listened to my kids. You followed textbook procedure over common sense and kept us stuck in this cycle instead of helping to set us free. You think you're so smart with your law degrees, black gowns, and expensive fees, but you're fools who were played by a manipulator—you're just like me. I'm agreeing to the settlement to get myself and my family the hell out of this system. So thank you very much, I'll manage my life and raise my kids from here. I'll do it from my gut, not from fear of my ex or the threat of this court. And I'll do a damn good job.*

I'd paused long enough that Bruce nervously glanced at me and gently patted the side of my leg.

"No," I finally answered, pouring all the emotion of my unspoken thoughts into my labored response.

We filed out into the hallway, and Jason disappeared like a phantom. It would be a few years before he disappeared for good.

"Good luck," Abe said to me sincerely. "Call me if you or the boys ever need anything."

"Thanks," I said. *I got it from here.*

"Thank you." I turned to Bruce, unable to find better words to express my appreciation. He'd shown up when I desperately needed him and guided me so I wouldn't need him forever.

"You're going to be okay. Don't engage with this guy," he offered as parting advice.

I smiled softly, not wanting him to leave me but understanding it was time he did.

I walked out toward my car and completely filled my lungs with fresh air for the first time in years. The sensation stunned me, like I'd just gotten up after being knocked over by a wave. I felt the relief of walking toward the shore, but the trauma left me unsteady.

"Miss." Jason's attorney gently tapped my arm.

I pulled back, startled, ready to defend myself.

"I hope everything works out for you." She sounded sincere.

We locked eyes and acknowledged each other, not as defendant and opposing counsel, but as people.

"Thank you," I said softly, happy to release some anger.

I continued toward my car, vaguely aware there was still a heaviness in my chest. It came as no surprise to find a parking ticket wedged under my windshield wiper. I looked up to the heavens. "Can I catch a break?" I laughed. I knew it was a sign that I still had issues to resolve before I could be at peace.

~

A few days after the final court appearance, I scuttled into Angela's office for my weekly appointment, excited to fill her in. I boasted about the resolution of the case, but deep down I wasn't satisfied. I kept retelling the story, blaming others for injustices inflicted on me, and pointing a finger at their sins, hoping to feel relief.

I rehashed the forensics bit. "She told me he's a sociopath!"

"There's no doubt in my mind what kind of person Jason is," she agreed.

I nodded and sat upright on the couch, unaware ten years of healing work was about to begin.

"So tell me," she asked, "why did you marry him?"

Francesca Miracola is an Italian American from Queens, NY, currently living on Long Island, but in her mind she's a free-spirited wanderer. She wants to travel the world, but she's afraid to fly, although a glass of wine gets her through most flights. Francesca's mostly an introvert who greatly prefers deep, meaningful conversations to surface small talk. She keeps her circle small, and she's still debating if that's a good or bad thing. She's a breast cancer survivor, but she rarely defines herself as one—probably because she feels like she's been surviving something most of her life. She's funny; at least, she makes herself laugh. Francesca graduated *cum laude* from New York University and worked in financial services for twenty-five years, even though she wanted to be a therapist. That's probably because she needed a therapist. Francesca finally wound up on her true path as a student and teacher of *A Course in Miracles*, author, life coach, and founder of Protagonist Within LLC. Francesca is a wife, a best friend, and above all, a mother. Visit her website at francescamiracola.com.